Pressed
Flower
DECORATIONS

Pressed Flower DECORATIONS

Margaret Spencer

Bobbs-Merrill Indianapolis New York

Published by The Bobbs-Merrill Company, Inc.
Indianapolis   New York

Published in Great Britain by Wm. Collins Sons & Co. Ltd.
ISBN 0-672-52061-3
Library of Congress Catalog Card Number: 74-11402

Manufactured in Great Britain
First U.S. printing 1975

CONTENTS

List of colour illustrations

Cover illustration: The flowers used in this lovely design are larkspur, cow parsley, hydrangea, bedstraw, daisy, heather, clary, limnanthes, silverweed, horseshoe vetch, quaking grass, senecio, statice, chrysanthemum haradjanii.

Wild Flowers

Before starting to pick wild flowers, you should check with your local Conservation Board as to which flowers are protected in your State.

The following is a list of brands which may be recommended for use with pressed flowers.

latex-based adhesive	Sobo
clear/coloured adhesive tape	{ Scotch Magic Tape { MMM Tape
extra-strong adhesive tape	{ Scotch { MMM extra-strong tape
transparent adhesive film	Dennison's Clear Seal
flocked adhesive film	flocked paper (a few colours have adhesive backing; most have to be used with Sobo)
transparent acrilic sheet	Plexiglass
adhesive putty	Hold-it
florist's foam blocks	{ Oasis { Fill-fast Foam
transparent lacquer	Valspar

INTRODUCTION

Have you considered making table mats with the daisies on your lawn? Or finger plates with buttercups and larkspur? It can be done and it is really quite simple.

In Victorian days, when all young ladies were expected to be able to paint and embroider and play the piano, the less talented at these accomplishments would press ferns and flowers and make them into pictures or use them to decorate portraits of their loved ones. Sadly, most of their work has now disappeared, but occasionally a faded picture or two can be found in a museum.

Nowadays, when people are once again turning to handcrafts for relaxation and pleasure, this pleasant Victorian pastime is becoming more and more popular. Young and old are discovering that it is an ideal craft to practise at home, since it does not require a great deal of study and there is no specialized or expensive equipment to buy. Indeed it was because pressed flower decorations could be made so easily and economically that I decided to take up the craft.

And what a very rewarding hobby it has turned out to be! Even now, after making hundreds of pictures and finger plates, I still get a thrill each time I start on a new decoration. In a world chock-full of mass-produced goods, there is tremendous personal satisfaction in creating something useful and attractive which cannot be found by the dozen in almost any shop. It is for this reason that I decided to write a book on the subject, for I want to share the enjoyment this craft has given me.

I imagine almost every schoolchild knows how to press flowers between sheets of blotting paper, but in the following chapters I hope to show how you can preserve them to make delightful articles which you can sell, or give to your friends or keep to brighten up your home.

Do not worry if garden flowers are difficult to come by, it is still possible to make lovely decorations with leaves and wild flowers gathered from the wayside on a Sunday afternoon stroll. Try experimenting with any flowers you can find, for although in Chapter 2 I give a list of what to press, there are many flowers I have not yet tested.

Once you have mastered the simple techniques of pressing and sticking down, there are lots of different ways you can use your flowers. A picture or finger plate would make a charming gift for a homesick expatriate, and what grandparent would not be thrilled to receive a home-grown calendar or bookmark at Christmas time? Wall hangings and table mats sell well at bazaars, and a lampshade or firescreen decorated with holiday pressings makes a lovely and unusual souvenir.

This is a hobby all the family can share, so, if you love flowers and would like to create something original and attractive, you will find it a happy pastime and great fun!

Note
It should be appreciated that the term pressed flowers covers not only the actual blooms, but any part of the plant which can be preserved by pressing, such as leaves, stalks, seedheads and tendrils.

1 BEAUTY PRESERVED

And this same flower that smiles today,
Tomorrow will be dying.

So wrote the poet Robert Herrick, and this, alas, is only too true unless we take steps to preserve that smile. With many flowers this can be done quite simply by pressing them between sheets of absorbent paper, then later, when they are quite dry, they can be made into pictures and other decorations so that they may smile today, tomorrow and all the year round.

To many people the term pressed flowers suggests only an uninspiring picture of faded blooms and dead-looking leaves, for many still remember the rather dreary pressings of their early schooldays, and, therefore, find it hard to visualize how colourful and exciting pressed material can be, if it is picked and preserved correctly.

Once, when I was exhibiting some of my pictures and finger plates, a lady remarked, "I would never have imagined pressed flowers could look so *alive*. They are just as attractive as fresh ones".

This is not an unusual experience. People are often surprised at the beauty and adaptability of pressed flowers, and I very rarely show my work without being asked, "How do you get your preserved material to look so natural? Could I do it?" I always answer, "Yes, of course you could; anyone can do it. All you need is a little know-how and time and patience".

These last two requirements are every bit as important as the first. For this is no instant hobby. It takes time to press flowers and make them into decorations, and it needs patience to preserve them successfully. In some cases it may take five or six weeks for the material to dry out completely, and during the all-important first four weeks of this period they must not be disturbed in any way, which means there can be no peeping to see how things are getting on!

Yet, although the drying process takes several weeks, the other stages—picking, pressing and designing can be fitted in to odd moments of the day, a little at a time.

It takes only a few minutes to pick and press sufficient flowers and foliage to decorate a door finger plate, and another forty minutes or so to design and complete it. In between there will, of course, have been the long wait for the material to dry out, but it will have taken less than an hour of your time to capture a little bit of summer and create with it a lovely decoration which you and your family can enjoy for years to come.

You can begin pressing material in early spring, when the first ash and oak leaves appear, and gradually build up a collection of flowers, leaves and grasses throughout the summer and autumn. Then, when winter comes, you will have a hoard of exciting material hidden away in your pressing books, all ready for you to make into Christmas presents or useful decorations for your home.

PICKING FOR PRESSING

There is a wide variety of flowers and foliage which can be preserved to make pressed flower decorations, and even if your garden cannot supply all you require, the countryside can. Collecting suitable material is one of the joys of this hobby, because it takes you out and about and opens your eyes to a host of things you have never really noticed before.

A stroll round the garden takes on a new significance when you are looking for flowers for your pictures, and a day in the country offers fresh delights, for here you can stock up with material which costs nothing but a little time and effort. In autumn even the city parks turn into happy hunting grounds for lovely frost-burnt leaves.

Once you become interested in this hobby, scissors, boxes and bags will accompany you on every outing for who knows what fresh treasure you may suddenly come across? But please remember when you are collecting wild flowers that they must not be *wasted*. Pick only a very few and allow the rest to grow and increase so that others may enjoy them too. There is more to flower-gathering than simply picking at random. Space your picking and move from plant to plant, taking only one or two flowers from each one. Bear in mind that it is quality that counts, not quantity.

WHEN TO PICK

Picking flowers for pressing is rather like picking vegetables for the freezer, both must be gathered at the right time for good results. In fact, timing is *the* most important factor for successful pressing. Each flower and leaf, except when they are required for cartoons, should be picked when it is at its best. Even an hour or two can spell the difference between success and failure. Take the little lawn daisy for example. If it is picked too early in the morning it is likely to lose its colour and dry out a drab-looking fawn. This is because the flower is still damp with dew, but, if it is picked late in the afternoon, the petals will have begun to close up for the night and it will then be difficult to get them to press out smoothly. However, if daisies are picked around midday, in full sunlight, they will press perfectly and retain their colour.

Some flowers are best gathered when they are just fully open, whilst others, such as larkspur and montbretia, can be pressed when they are still in bud. Foliage, too, needs care. Some leaves, such as those of the eccremocarpus should only be pressed when they are young and tender. These immature leaves will then turn black and look very striking indeed, but if they are pressed when they are older both leaves and tendrils dry out a dreary greenish-brown.

Timing is also very important when you are collecting grasses. They should be picked as soon as the heads are fully open, before the seeds have formed. A finger plate or table mat can so easily be spoilt by a few stray grass seeds, and, unfortunately, these seldom appear until after the edges have been sealed, when their removal becomes an extremely fiddly job.

Material for pressing should, ideally, be picked only on a dry, sunny day. *Never* pick after it has been raining. Wait a full twenty-four hours for the flowers to dry out completely. If they are even the slightest bit damp when put in the pressing books, they will lose their colour, or become spotted and mouldy and in either case you will have wasted time and energy, flowers and blotting paper. So be patient! Timing must be judged carefully, but fortunately the ability to do this is soon acquired.

KEEPING FLOWERS FRESH

How you gather your material and the way you look after it before it reaches the pressing book is most important. Freshness is essential. Do not expect a dying bloom to make a miraculous recovery while it is lying in its blotting paper bed, because it will not. Once flowers begin to wilt and shrivel, nothing will revive them, and so it is necessary to take steps to ensure that the material you collect remains as fresh and firm as possible.

This will present no problem if you are gathering the flowers from your own garden for they can go straight into the pressing books as soon as they are picked. However, it is a good idea to carry a box or basket around with you so that each flower you pick can be put into it as it is cut. I find that an ordinary kitchen colander is very useful when I am collecting short stemmed flowers such as pansies and lawn daisies.

Choose your material carefully, and pick only a few flowers at a time. This is particularly important when you are gathering limnanthes and daisies. These must be put into the pressing books as quickly as possible otherwise they will begin to close up. Pick about thirty or so flowers and press them immediately, then go back and pick another batch.

Collecting wild flowers calls for a different method altogether, unless, of course, you are lucky enough to have some growing almost on your doorstep. For most people it will probably mean travelling quite some distance, yet the material must be kept fresh during the journey home. Unfortunately wild flowers do not stay fresh as long as cultivated ones, so, unless you can ensure that they will reach your pressing book in really first class condition, it is best to leave them alone, particularly if the weather is very hot.

Flowers wilt because of loss of moisture and they lose it very rapidly when held in a hot hand, therefore standard equipment on any collecting trip must be polythene bags, a covered tin or plastic food box and a bucket or basket. The bags and boxes should be large enough to hold your flowers without crushing them and still leave plenty of space for air to circulate around them.

As you pick your flowers put them into the bag stems first. Do not gather too many, it is better to limit your collection to just a few flowers rather than collect too many and spoil most of them. When everything is in the bag, blow into it to inflate it, then fasten the top securely. The bag should then be stood in the bucket or hung up so that the blooms will not get squashed by the weight of material.

If you think you will not have time to press your flowers as soon as you get them home, it is a good plan to soak a block of florist's foam before setting out. Place the foam in the bottom of the polythene bag and push the flower stems into the damp block as you gather them. Blow into the bag so that the air will cushion the contents and close the top tightly. Material treated in this way will remain fresh for a much longer period. An hour or so before you start pressing, open the bag and roll the top right down so that any moisture which may have collected on the blooms can dry off.

Top *Some of the equipment needed when collecting flowers*
Bottom *Flowers keep fresh longer in florist's foam and an inflated plastic bag*

Leaves and grasses packed in a tin

Leaves and grasses can be packed one on top of another in the tin or box, and again it is important to leave plenty of room for a layer of air between the material and the lid.

Try to prevent the sun shining on your flowers while you are transporting them. A sheet of damp newspaper placed over the bags and boxes will help to shade them and keep them cool.

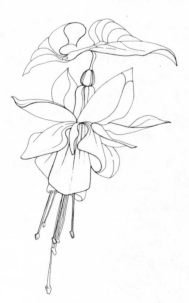

Not all flowers and leaves will press successfully. In some cases this is due to the texture of the material and in others to loss of colour when dry. It is not always the most colourful flower that makes the best presser. Unfortunately many beginners are inclined to pick only the bright blue and red flowers, unaware that most blues fade to a pale nothingness and most reds turn a dreary beige. So to avoid disappointment, and wasted flowers, I have listed the names of some tried and trusted friends of mine.

In some cases I have also given growing instructions, because, if you can grow some of your own flowers, your interest and enjoyment in pressing them will be greatly increased. There is something very satisfying about using home-grown materials, and by growing the plants in your own garden you have the advantage of being able to pick the flowers at exactly the right time for a successful pressing.

I realize I am lucky to have a large garden in which to grow most of the material I require, but it is not strictly necessary, for many of the plants I recommend here can be grown in an odd corner, in tubs and boxes or even in pots on the windowsill. If space is limited, then give priority to foliage plants, for flowers can be bought if necessary, but it is with stalks and leaves that decorations are designed and filled in.

None of the plants I have listed here are fussy about soil, etc. All the attention they need is to be kept well-watered when the weather is dry and to be given an occasional feed of fertilizer.

GARDEN FLOWERS

Alyssum saxatile Pull off small pieces and press flowers, leaves and stalks together. The flowers do not keep their bright yellow colour for very long, but they look so dainty that they are well worth touching up (see Chapter 4). These flowers look especially attractive when they are used on a dark background.

Anaphalis Press the crisp, pearly-white flowers only. These can also be dried by tying the flowers, leaves and stalks into bunches and hanging upside down in a warm room. When dry, nip off the flowers and remove the fluffy seedheads from the centres, then press the flowers for one or two days to flatten them. You can make a false centre with a mimosa bobble or you can use the reverse side of the flower, in which case a centre is not necessary.

Anthemis This yellow, daisy-like flower is excellent for colour retention. *Tinctoria kelwayi* is a pretty lemon coloured variety, and *Sancti-Johannis* has golden-yellow flowers. These flowers *must* be picked at the correct time, which is about 2–3 days after opening. If left until all the tiny florets in the middle have opened, it will be impossible to press it without losing most of the petals. Press the stalk separately, preferably in a curve.

Christmas rose Pick in early spring while still white. Cut off the flower and press whole under a very heavy weight. It will dry out a lovely creamy-white and make a charming focal point for a large picture or firescreen with a dark background.

Chrysanthemum, annual Press whole flowers under a fairly heavy weight. Some varieties may need touching up (see Chapter 4).

Clematis Jackmanni Pull apart and press each petal separately. Use both sides of the petals in a design, the dark topside and the paler reverse side.

Clematis Mme. Edouard André and **Ville de Lyon**   Both these varieties have deep carmine flowers which dry out a maroon colour. Pull apart and press each petal separately. These varieties need fairly heavy pressing.

Clematis viticella   Press the little navy and white buds together with their stalks and any small leaves.

Cosmos   Use the single variety only. Press whole flowers.

Daffodil   Cut off stalk and seedbox then cut in two lengthways, leaving three petals and half the trumpet in each half, so that one daffodil makes two separate flowers (see illustration below).

Delphinium   Pick only when the weather has been dry for at least two days. You can either cut off the spikes and press whole flowers, or dismantle the flowers and press each petal separately. If the weather has been hot and dry, it will be safe to press the flowers in their entirety, but, if it has been the least bit damp, it is safer to press them petal by petal.

Freesia   Press unopened, yellow and orange buds.

Fuchsia   Press flowers, unopened buds and flower stems, but not the leaves. So far I have only tested the common hardy varieties, *Magellancia* and *Riccartonii*, with the red and purple flowers. Press only when there has been at least two dry days.

Gaillardia   Pull off each petal and press separately, reassemble when dry.

Gazania   Pull off each petal and press separately. Also press the dark green leaves. Gazania petals are very fragile, so you should use only the smallest dot of adhesive on the lower tip of each petal when using them in a decoration. Use the undersides of the leaves on a dark background.

Heather   Do not press the very hard stalks. Break off small pieces and press separately.

Heuchera   Press only the coral-pink and crimson varieties. The flowers and stems should be pressed together. These flowers look very dainty when used in a design with silver-grey leaves.

A daffodil cut in two lengthwise

Honeysuckle This needs heavy pressing. Pick off every floret, including the tiny buds, and press them separately. Re-assemble when dry. Honeysuckle dries out a deep beige colour, but because of its shape, still looks very attractive and is a must for cartoons.

Hydrangea Press each floret separately. Many will dry out beige or green, but the deep pink ones are useful for dotting among silver leaves.

Larkspur This is one of my favourites. Press a good supply of it for it is one of the best flowers for keeping its colour. Remove flowers and unopened buds from their stems and press separately. I think the flowers stand out better if the stamens are removed before pressing. Press some flowers full face and some side face.

To grow Larkspur, sow in September for early flowering in the following year, or in March and April for flowering in July to September. The site should be well dug and the seedlings thinned out to about one foot apart. The deep blue and purple varieties are the best for pressing and under the right conditions will retain their colour for many years. Height 2½–3 feet (760–910 mm).

Limnanthes Nip off stalks and press flowers and stalks separately. These 'fried egg' flowers keep their colours well and look very pretty on a black background. Press some stalks in a curve.

Mimosa This can be purchased from the florists. Gently pull each little frond off the main stem and see that some are pressed in a curve. After about a year the bobbles turn a burnt orange colour. Press under a very heavy weight. Discard the leaves.

Montbretia Press flowers and buds. The open flowers should be pressed separately.

Plant in spring, four inches (102 mm) deep and three inches (76 mm) apart, in well drained soil. It is fairly hardy, but in heavy soils and cold districts it should be covered with a layer of peat, bracken or leaf mould during the winter months. The flowers grow on 12–15 inch (300–380 mm) stems and, like larkspur, will retain their colour for a good many years. If the plants are happy, they will soon spread into clumps which should be divided every three or four years. Best for pressing is the pure orange strain.

Pansy Press only the flowers and select strains with 'faces', since the clear varieties soon fade. The best for colour retention are the bright yellow, deep crimson and wine-purple.

Pansies can be grown from seed sown in well drained soil in a partially shaded position, or plants can be bought from the nurseryman ready for planting out. The advantage in buying plants is that they are usually in flower and so you can select the more vivid and best marked specimens. They do quite well in pots and tubs but you should not allow them to go to seed as this shortens their flowering life considerably. Height between 6 and 9 inches (152 and 229 mm).

Passion flower Press flowers, stigmas and stamens only. Needs a heavy pressing.

Potentilla Press the brilliant magenta-rose flowers only.

Primula auricula Press the deep mauve sort only. Pull the flower-heads from the stalks so that the calyx and stamens come

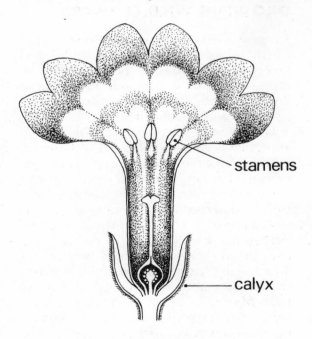

This drawing shows the calyx and stamens in a Primula auricula. They should be pulled off with the flower head

15

away too, then press the flowers quickly before the petals have a chance to curl up. Discard stalks, calyx and stamens.

Primula polyanthus Press the red variety only. This turns a deep mauvy-brown. Do not press leaves or stalks.

Rose All roses turn cream or beige after a time, so this is one of the flowers I cheat with (see Touching up, Chapter 4). Press only the very small old-fashioned red roses and small red ramblers. Press flowers only, under a heavy weight.

Rudbeckia Pull off petals and press separately. Use to make 'mock' flowers or re-assemble with a false centre. Most varieties press well.

Statice Hang up to dry. When dried out, pull off some tiny florets and press for a day or two before using in a decoration. Can be used to make mock flowers.

Tulips Press each petal separately. The yellow-red and black parrot variety are the best for pressing.

Ursinia Press complete flowers. These petals are very fragile so need careful handling.

GROWING WILD FLOWERS

In most gardens there is an odd corner which can be turned into a little wild flower garden. To some people it may be just a patch of weeds, but to the keen flower presser it can be a constant source of attractive and valuable material.

On one of our rock banks, *Wild pansies* grow alongside the more usual rock plants. I discovered a root growing in the vegetable garden a few years ago, and found the tiny flowers to be such good pressers that I decided it deserved a less humble abode and so I moved it to the bank outside the kitchen window. Some of the flowers were left to seed themselves, and I now have a dozen or so plants each year which produce an almost continuous supply of blooms from May right up to November. I have found that the poorer the soil, the smaller the flowers will be, so I now grow one or two little pansies in a corner of the drive-way. These produce very dark minute flowers which are perfect for small articles

Plate 1

Top left   *Roses in the garden*

Top right   *A page of Delphinium heads and petals prepared for pressing.*

Centre right   *This shows examples of Roses before and after fading, and after being touched up.*

Bottom   *Poster paints can be mixed to give a wide variety of shades and tints, as shown here.*

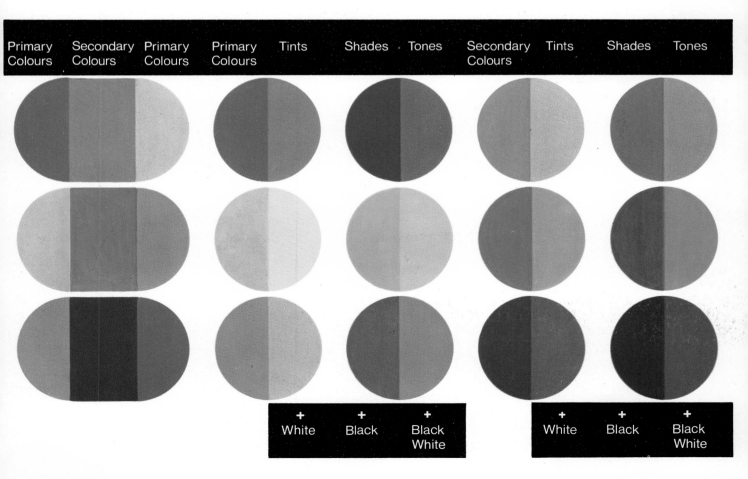

Primary Colours	Secondary Colours	Primary Colours	Primary Colours	Tints	Shades	Tones	Secondary Colours	Tints	Shades	Tones

| | | | + White | + Black | + Black White | | | + White | + Black | + Black White |

Plate 2

This picture could be hung either horizontally or vertically. The Passion flower has an orange Anaphalis centre to make it stand out a little more. I coloured a spray of these flowers by dipping them in some orange dye and then hung them up to dry. The three tiny Polyanthus to the bottom left of the passion flower are particular favourites of mine because they have an equally attractive green and brown reverse side.

such as bookmarks, finger plates and light switch surrounds.

My own wild garden is a sunny, stony patch behind the greenhouse. Here I have planted *Silverweed, Herb Robert* and *Cow parsley* as all these will grow well on poor soil. The cow parsley has to be kept under control, but the silverweed and herb Robert are allowed to spread along the entire length of the greenhouse, where the various shades of red, white, green and silver mingle prettily and bring welcome colour to this rather drab corner of the garden. The silverweed has grown from two roots I dug up from a farm gateway, and the herb Robert and cow parsley from seed gathered on a country walk.

We have a small paddock on one side of our garden where I keep a few ducks. Here *Buttercups, Clover, Ladies bedstraw, Trefoil* and *Ox-eye daisies* are encouraged to grow. Fortunately ducks are not as destructive as hens, they do not scratch up plants and wallow in dust baths and so, apart from the occasional squashed buttercup, the flowers are quite undamaged.

Had I not got the paddock, all these plants could have been grown in the wild garden where they would have done equally well as they grow in any ordinary soil.

PRESSING WILD FLOWERS

Buttercup These are the easiest of all flowers to press. Flowers, stalks, leaves and buds should all be pressed together. Press some flowers side face (see page 18).

Celandine Pick and press only a few flowers at a time as they close up very quickly. Pick in full sunlight, and use on a dark background as they turn white in about a year.

Cinquefoils, Tormentil and **Spring cinquefoil** Press the small yellow flowers only. These do not keep their colour for long so this is another of the flowers I cheat with (see Touching up, Chapter 4).

Clover Press only the white variety. The flower fades to a rather dull beige colour but is well worth pressing because of its shape. It is particularly useful when its stalk has

17

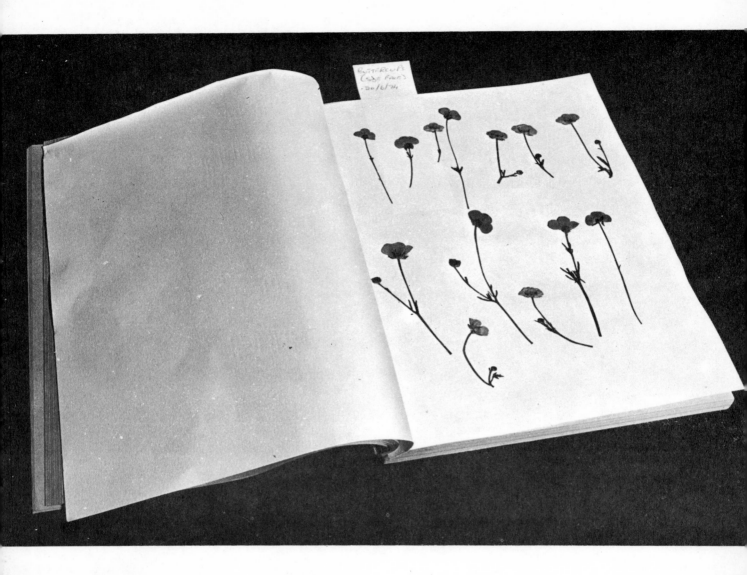

Press buttercups whole, both full and side face. Notice how they are spaced out on the page

been pressed in a curve. This flower should have its whirly middle highlighted with a little white or dark green poster paint (see Chapter 4).

Cow parsley This is one of the most useful flowers and looks very attractive when it is arranged on a dark background. Press whole flowers, but only press the leaves when they have turned purple (see Chapter 4).

Horseshoe vetch Press flowers, leaves and stalks together. Although the leaves turn beige after a time, they are very neat and have an interesting shape so are worth pressing. The flowers dry out green, yellow or a deep cream and keep their colour for a number of years.

Ladies bedstraw Do not press the woody part of the stalk. Remove pieces and press them separately. It dries out black and looks very dainty, and is therefore excellent for filling-in on finger plates and other small decorations.

Lawn daisy Pick in full sunlight before it closes up. Press flower and stalk together, and see that some flowers are pressed full face, and some side face. When you are designing, use some daisies with their reverse side uppermost. The dark green calyx is as pretty as the yellow centre (see Chapter 4).

The daisy is so widespread and abundant that I am sure you will have some growing somewhere in your garden, but if you plant one or two roots of the red double daisy, *Bellis perennis*, many of the wild daisies will become cross-pollinated and produce lovely pink or crimson-tipped petals. These modest little flowers bring a cheerful glow to all pressed flower decorations, especially finger plates and table mats.

Nipplewort Press this when it is just in bud, and then later when it is in seed. But do remember to remove all the seeds before pressing!

Ox-eye daisy Press flowers only and space them well out on the blotting paper. These need to be pressed under a fairly heavy weight (see Chapter 4).

Plantain Press the spikes only, before they flower, when they are blackish-brown. Plantains need a heavy pressing and are useful where a good bold line is required.

Silverweed Press the silvery leaves only.

Wild pansy Flowers can be yellow, violet or both. Snip off their heads and press them all!

Wild parsnip This looks rather like yellow cow parsley and is treated in the same way. Press the flowers and any purple leaves (see Chapter 4).

Woodruff Press as for ladies bedstraw.

You will notice that I have not included any of the rarer wild flowers in this list. This is because I feel these species should be protected and left to multiply. In some areas wild flowers have almost disappeared. They have either been sprayed or mown down before they could re-seed themselves, or dug up and destroyed as more and more fields come under the plough. Many of us could help save and even increase these plants by collecting the seeds and re-sowing them in our gardens, around playing fields and on neglected plots of land. After all, great efforts are being made to preserve our old buildings, so now we must help conserve the simple wild flowers that have

brightened our lanes and wastelands for so long.

LEAVES AND STEMS

Ash Press large and small leaves and the identical pair growing at the ends of the young shoots. Ash leaves dry out black.

Beech If pressed when very young the leaves will dry a pale lemony-green. Also press the leaves in autumn when they are 'turning'.

Blackberry Press these in autumn when they are crimson and gold.

Broom Press unflowered shoots. These dry out black or a very dark brown and look most effective when used on lampshades.

Cineraria centuria Press all the small silver leaves.

Clary This is an annual and is easily grown from seed sown in the spring. It will grow almost anywhere and makes a bushy plant about one and a half feet (457 mm) tall. The flowers are very insignificant, the attraction lying in the leaves. These can be pink, purple, blue, or white and can be used to form a base for pictures and finger plates, and also to make 'mock' flowers. Press each leaf separately.

Clematis montana This climber is also worth growing if you have room for it. The leaves and stems dry out black and are indispensable wherever a strong line is required. Do not press the flowers, they turn a pale fawn and look rather insipid.

It needs plenty of space and should be given a wall to itself, as it is far too vigorous to share it with another plant. Young pot-grown plants are available from most nurserymen and can be transplanted at any time between September and May. It will thrive in a well prepared and well drained soil provided the roots are shaded by some low shrubs or herbaceous plants. Prune established plants in June by cutting out the old flowering-stems and tying in the new shoots to form a framework.

Cotinus Press in the autumn when the leaves have turned a mixture of deep pink and purple. These leaves are useful where a smooth, clean outline is required.

Eccremocarpus This climber is a must for all pressed flower artists! It will grow well up the wall of a house, trellis, pillar, or even up and along a hedge. It is covered in lovely tubular red or orange flowers from early spring until cut down by winter frosts. Unfortunately the flowers are not good pressers, but the young leaves and tendrils more than make up for this, in fact I have never had a bad pressing with this plant, but the leaves must be young and on the small side. They then turn black and are invaluable for giving line and movement to a design.

It is a hardy plant and will do well almost anywhere so long as it has plenty of light. It is self-seeding and once established will provide you with dozens of spare plants. The seed pods themselves are most attractive and look rather like rows of little green lanterns. When dry they can be painted with white, gold or silver paint to make a charming addition to the Christmas decorations or dried flower arrangements.

Echinops The flowers can be dried but they are not suitable for pressing. The spear-like leaf is a lovely green on top and blue-grey underneath, and can be pressed in the usual way, or ironed dry. To do this, the leaf should be placed between sheets of blotting paper and pressed with a cool iron for five or ten minutes.

Goosegrass This dries out almost black and makes a good strong line.

Herb Robert Press leaves and stems when they have turned red.

Honeysuckle Press leaves and thin stalks. These will turn a very dark brown.

Ivy Press plenty of very small leaves. They make a nice base for a design on a finger plate.

Japanese maple Press in spring, summer and autumn.

Oak Press when leaves are young and a pinky-red colour. These will dry brown. *Turkey oak* leaves can be pressed in a slight curve.

Primrose Press the stalks only in a curve. Do not press the flowers, these fade badly.

Prunus Press in autumn.

Raspberry Press large and small leaves. Use the silver-grey undersides only. The top side turns beige after a few months.

Senecio cineraria This is well worth growing as the serrated silvery leaves look most attractive in the herbaceous border and they make excellent 'hands' for cartoon people. The unopened buds press well too, and can be pulled from the cluster so that each bud has a little curly grey stalk. Grow as for Senecio greyii. It is fairly hardy, but to be on the safe side pot up a few plants and bring inside for the winter. It grows to a height of about two feet (610 mm).

Senecio greyii This hardy plant has silvery stems and grey-green leaves which are creamy-white on the underside. The flowers, which look like small yellow daisies, are no good for pressing, but the leaves and clusters of unopened buds press perfectly and stand out well on a dark background. You can use either side of the leaves in a design.

Cuttings of this plant root easily, so you can grow a succession of bushes and discard the old ones when the stems become thick and woody. Plant in an ordinary soil in April, preferably in a sunny position. It grows to a height of about three feet (914 mm).

Thalictrum Press leaves when they have turned to red and yellow. You can also press the empty seedheads.

Virginia creeper Press in autumn when the leaves have changed colour.

Whitebeam Use the silver-grey underside of the leaf.

Wisteria Use the leaf stems only. In December, when the wisteria has shed its leaves you will find hundreds of leaf stems lying on the ground below. The majority will be beautifully curved, so gather up all the very thin stems and spread them out to dry on sheets of newspaper in a warm room. When quite dry, flatten the stems by laying them on a thick newspaper and rolling each individual stem flat with the end of a rolling-pin.

When designing with thick stalks, such as honeysuckle and wisteria, you should dip a fine paint brush in some mild disinfectant and brush it over the stalks a few hours before sticking them down. This will prevent mildew forming.

GRASSES

Most grasses are worth pressing. The three listed below are favourites of mine.

Quaking grass Alas, due to the widespread use of sprays and our obsession with keeping verges tidy this attractive grass is quickly disappearing from the countryside. You can, however, buy packets of seed of the ornamental variety (giant quaking grass), *Briza maxima,* and these should be sown in pots or boxes in a sunny corner at anytime from March to May. Water once a day if the weather is warm, and thin out the seedlings if they are growing too closely together. Cut the grasses as soon as the heads are fully open. They are very dainty and small pieces can be removed and used for filling in. Press the stalk in a curve.

Wild barley Press in one piece and dismantle the whiskers as and when they are required.

Barren brome Press in one piece, then pull off heads with stalks attached.

FERNS

All ferns turn a golden brown after a time, but they are worth pressing as they can look very striking when they are used with the yellow and orange tones of mimosa, montbretia and anthemis.

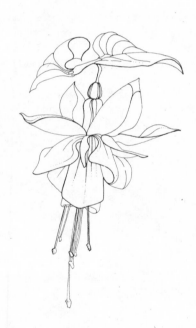

3 **HOW TO PRESS**

THE EQUIPMENT YOU NEED

One of the advantages of this hobby is that probably you will have most of the equipment you require for pressing flowers already. You will not have to rush out and buy any special tools before you begin, since the few items you need to start with will almost certainly be found around the house. Later, when you have acquired a little more experience, you may wish to press a greater quantity of material, in which case it will be necessary to obtain one or two additional pieces of equipment.

What, then, do you need in order to start? Well, first you will require some sheets of blotting paper or extra strong tissues. These must be quite smooth with no crinkles which could be transferred onto the leaves and petals, for nothing looks worse than a wrinkled, badly pressed flower. If you have neither blotting paper nor tissues in the house, you can make do with sheets of absorbent toilet paper or thick, paper table napkins.

Children usually find blotting paper the easiest to use, and although the initial outlay for a supply of blotting paper is considerably more than for tissues, the blotting paper can be re-used time and time again, if it is handled with care and dried out thoroughly after each pressing.

Next you will need some fairly thick books. Old wallpaper books or telephone directories make excellent pressing books. Most decorator's shops have out of date wallpaper pattern books which they will usually let you have. You will also require some bricks or other heavy objects to weight down the books, and a rolling-pin to smooth out the petals and flatten down the flower centres.

An old tie or trouser press can also be used for pressing flowers, and some of the larger craft shops now sell a special flower press. These screw presses are not essential, but they are useful for pressing flowers with thick centres, such as anthemis or ox-eye daisy. However, the flowers must not be left in the press indefinitely or they may go mouldy, so after three or four days they should be placed between fresh sheets of absorbent paper and transferred to the pressing books to finish drying out.

TECHNIQUE

Before starting to press your flowers you must first make sure that they have no inhabitants, either dead or alive! Go over them carefully and remove any foreign matter you find. Once they are pressed it will be difficult to do this without damaging the blooms.

Unless the stalk is a thin one, it is best to snip off the flower and press it separately. Place the flowers on a sheet of blotting paper or extra strong tissue and flatten the centres with your thumb, taking great care to spread all the petals out evenly and smoothly. Then press the stalks separately and, if there are any buds or attractive seedheads, press these at the same time. Do not overcrowd the flowers, space them out so that they are not touching each other.

Flowers with a hard centre, such as honeysuckle, clematis and rudbeckia, should have their petals removed and pressed individually. The middles can be discarded, then, when the petals are pressed and dried, they can be reassembled exactly as they grew with a false centre made from another flower.

When you have filled one sheet of blotting paper, cover the flowers with another sheet and give them a light roll with your

Left *No expensive equipment is needed when pressing flowers*

Below *Flatten the flower heads and spread the petals evenly*

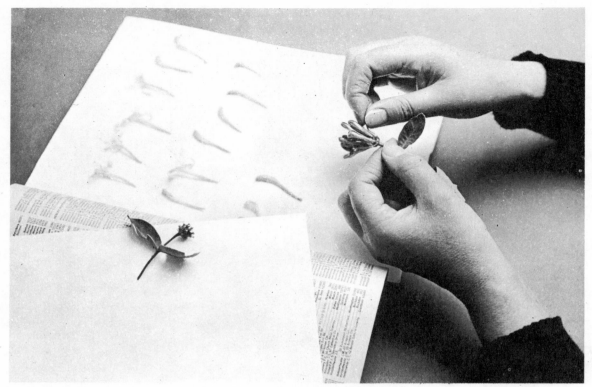

Above   *Pulling the petals off honeysuckle to press separately*

Below   *Rolling the flowers between sheets of blotting paper to give them a good start*

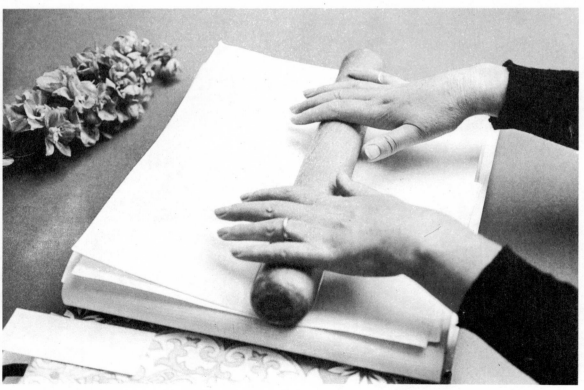

Above *Weigh down the pressing book very firmly*

Below *Press stalks and grasses in natural curves*

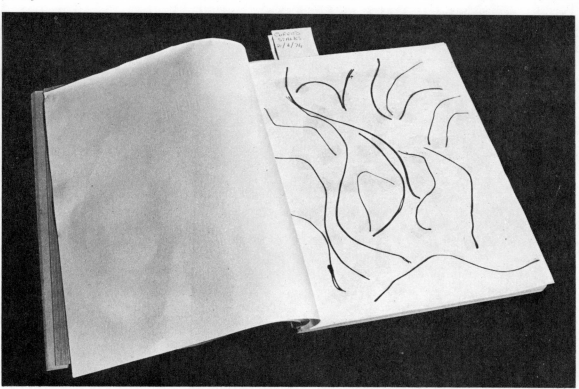

rolling-pin to get them off to a good start. Now place the blotting paper sandwich between the pages of a thick book, as close to the spine as possible, and weigh down with several bricks or more books.

If you are using a wallpaper book with washable or vinyl coated paper, you should place your pressings between the *reverse* side of the patterns as these will be more absorbent.

Leaves are pressed in the same way, but stalks and grasses should be pressed in a curve. Try to avoid poker-straight lines. Look at the flowers and foliage in your garden, if you have one, and emulate their gentle twists and turns.

When you are pressing clovers, snip off the flowers and press them separately, then place the stalks in a shallow jar without any water. In an hour or so they will have begun to droop into attractive curves and you can then press them in the usual way. Other supple stalks can be pressed in a curved position with the aid of a few strips of adhesive tape.

When placing material inside the pressing book, remember to leave about five pages between each sandwich. If pressings are too close together, they will not lie flat and this can easily spoil the flowers.

It is essential to press firmly, so weight the books down well then leave them undisturbed for at least five or six weeks. The pressing books should be stored in a damp-free, well-ventilated room, away from hot fires or radiators. If the room is more than 65°F the flowers may dry out too quickly and become brittle and difficult to handle. When you are using a number of pressing books it is a good idea to change them around every week or so. Move the bottom books to the top of the pile, and the top ones to the bottom. This allows all the pressings an occasional breather and prevents them from going musty.

After about six weeks, when the pressing and drying process has been completed, you will be able to look through your books and see how your flowers have turned out. I love doing this and get as excited as a child opening a Christmas stocking, for one never really knows what one will find. The colours of the flowers are not always as bright when pressed as they were when growing, and in some cases they will have changed completely. For example, a deep red polyanthus will turn a lovely mauvy-brown when dry, and bright green ladies bedstraw turns almost black (see plate 5). Often, too, flowers which have retained their colours well one year, will fade or turn mouldy in another. So many things can influence a pressing. Much depends on the age of the flowers and the state of the weather, not only on the day they were gathered, but in the preceding weeks. Then again, the actual pressing itself and the storage play an important part. It is this uncertainty, this little gamble, which makes the hobby so fascinating and adds a touch of excitement to every opening of the pressing book.

NAME TAGS

Each time you place a floral sandwich between the pages of your pressing book write out a name tag, stating the name of the flowers or leaves in the sandwich, and the date they were pressed. This should stick out of the book like a bookmark and it will save a great deal of time in the months to come when you are looking for special flowers for your decorations.

If you intend pressing a large amount of material, it is a good idea to use separate books, say one for yellow and orange flowers, another for red, blue and purple and a third for white and in-between shades. The many attractive silvery-grey buds and leaves could also be kept in a separate book, and the brown, black and autumn tinted leaves in another. Stalks and grasses should have a book of their own too, and very often, simply by looking at a page of delicately curving stalks, you will get an idea for a design for a picture or finger plate.

Do remember to include the pressing date on the name tags. Flowers can sometimes look dry and well pressed after only ten days in the pressing book, but it will not be safe to use them for at least another two or three weeks. So to avoid mistakes, you must note dates.

Efficient use of name tags saves time and effort later on

FLOWERS FROM LOOSE PETALS

If some of the flowers which you have pressed have not turned out too well, do not throw them away. Save the good parts for mock flowers. The centres can be used to replace those extra hard clematis and rudbeckia middles which you discarded, and the petals can be made into some pretty and original flowers (see page 28).

Eight dark blue delphinium petals arranged around a lawn daisy make a *Delphaisy*, and five rudbeckia petals and one anaphalis flower become an *Anabeckia*.

These loose petals can also form a very handy section of spares, which can be a godsend when you have to repair a faulty or slightly damaged flower. Sometimes, on close inspection, an otherwise perfect bloom will show a small blemish on one petal. With the aid of a spot of glue and a spare petal this can soon be put right and no one but you need ever know that it was less than perfect (see pages 28–30).

Single petals, surplus middles and malpressed leaves are specially useful for collage cartoons, but I will tell you more about this in Chapter 9.

Above *New flowers from old: left Ana-*
beckia, right Delphaisy   Below *Two flowers with damaged petals*

Above   *Spare petals to replace damaged*   Below   *Applying the glue*
ones

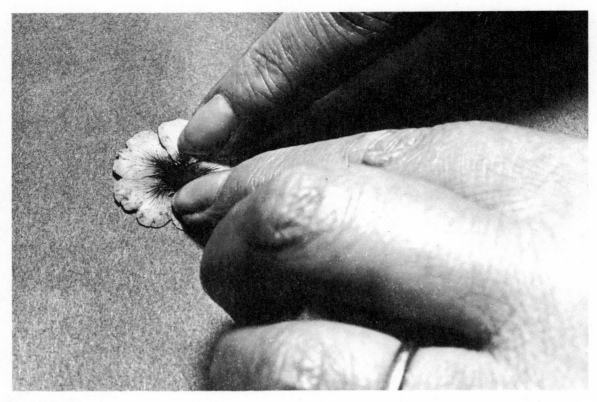

Above   *Positioning a replacement petal*   Below   *The 'repaired' flower*

Above and Below *When testing new pressers for colour retention glue them on* *cardboard, cover with transparent film and hang in the light for a year*

TESTING FLOWERS

It is always exciting to discover a new presser, so if there are any attractive flowers or leaves growing in your garden or along the roadside which you think might be possible pressers, do experiment with them. All too often people say to me, "Oh, if only I had known that such and such a flower would press!" Yet by making a simple test they could easily have found out.

Material under test should be pressed in the usual way then, after about five or six weeks, when it is quite dry, it should be

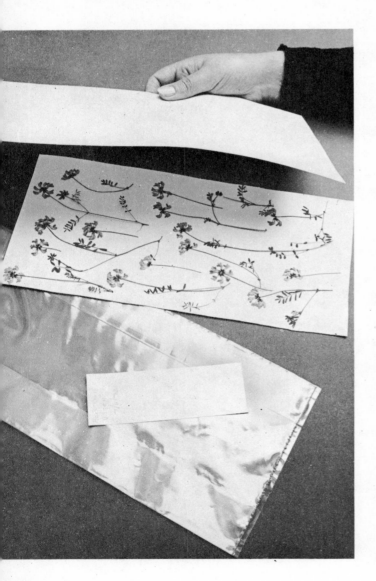

Plate 3
Top   *The two foliage Cinerarias used in this arrangement were grown in pots on the window-sill. This simple sparkling design has a feeling of grace and movement, and the silvery-white tones will add coolness to a room on summer days.*
Bottom   *This is one of the rare occasions when I have used a fabric background with pressed flowers. I found this scrap of midnight-blue velvet in the bottom of my work basket and decided it was just the right colour for a 'moon-lit' swan collage. When you are using a fabric background you must be extra careful with the sticking down operation. Use as little adhesive as possible so that it will not leak or smear, for it is extremely difficult to remove once it has soaked into the fabric.*

As you will see, the swan is made almost entirely of silver-toned leaves. In some places I have laid one leaf over another in order to get a shadowy effect. The eye is an Eccremocarpus leaflet and a knot of black thread, and the bill is a Senecio greyii leaf which I have coloured with a little orange paint. The water is made from more pieces of senecio leaf and some large white daisy petals which I have lightly tinted with eye shadow!

Plate 4
Left   *Four sprays of Mimosa and five Clary leaves make a nice wide base to this vertical 'mixture of all sorts'. This is one of the examples referred to on page 43.*
Right   *A lazy curve of Larkspur, Clary, Montbretia and Eccremocarpus leaves and tendrils. The golden-brown leaves at the base are Thalictrum. These were pressed in the autumn, when they were changing colour. The arrangement also includes Mimosa, Quaking grass and a single Polyanthus flower.*

Storing flowers
If necessary pressed flowers may be stored in polythene bags
Left   *Flowers being sandwiched between two sheets of blotting paper*

CALENDAR

Plate 5

Top left *The yellow, orange, white and silver tones in this finger plate show up well against the black background. The Anaphalis at the base of the arrangement has been dipped in orange dye and was once part of a dried flower arrangement.*

Top centre *As much as possible has been squeezed into this finger plate design. Three Ivy leaves form the compact base, and the dark Polyanthus flower and small purple Pansies carry the eye to the Delphinium and Ladies Bedstraw at the top.*

Top right *The Virginia creeper leaf makes a neat base in this finger plate. Plantains, Ladies bedstraw and Montbretia lead the eye outwards and upwards to the smaller Virginia creeper leaves.*

Bottom *Two attractive arrangements for table mats. The daisy-chain design is particularly popular.*

Plate 6

Top left *I have bent the rules a little with this Christmas card by colouring some small pieces of grass with red dye and spraying the Clematis stalk, empty Thalictrum seedheads and some of the Cow parsley with gold paint. Crimson Heuchera bells and Ivy leaves sprinkled with cow parsley snow complete the design.*

Top right *Eccremocarpus tendrils lead the eye from the small Pansy at the centre base up to the two pink-tipped Daisies at the centre top. The daisy-like flowers in the corners were pressed by a friend when she was on holiday. As they had already begun to fade a little, I have touched them up with poster paint.*

Bottom left *Note the little arrangement at the base of this calendar and the way the stalks and tendrils radiate out towards the edges. Each Larkspur floret was pressed separately then reassembled with the smallest flowers at the outer end of the stalk.*

Bottom right *The mauve Delphinium at the bottom of this tasselled wall hanging gives the arrangement a good sturdy base. Buttercups and Larkspur draw the eye to the Mimosa at the top.*

glued on to a piece of cardboard or a disposable plate and covered with some transparent adhesive film (see page 55). This test decoration can then be hung up in a light, airy room away from direct sunlight. If the flowers are still showing plenty of colour after twelve months or so, you will have discovered another good presser to add to my list! However, there is no need to be discouraged if they fade after only a few weeks. If it is a smallish flower and it has pressed out well, it may be worth touching

Below *Sliding the flowers into the polythene bag. The air should be removed from the bag and the top sealed*

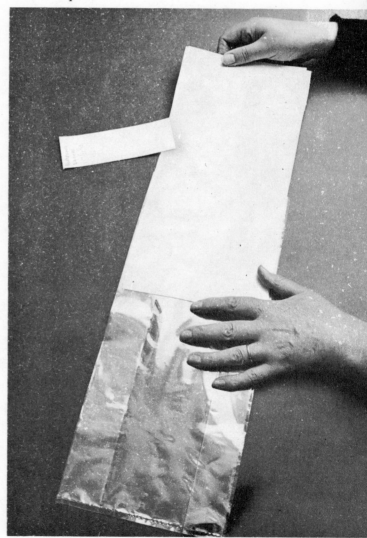

up in the way described in Chapter 4. Then again, if it has faded to a pretty creamy-white, perhaps it could be placed on a purple cotinus leaf where it will show up well against the leaf's dark background.

Always test at least six flowers or leaves of each new variety. This will allow for one or two of them fading simply because they were not picked at the right stage of their development.

A brand new presser can set one's inspiration flowing, so always be on the lookout for something different.

STORING FLOWERS

Some people like to take their flowers out of the pressing books as soon as they are pressed and dry so that they will have room to press more material, but I do not recommend this. Pressed material must be kept pressed and dry at all times, even when made into decorations, otherwise the leaves and petals begin to wrinkle, and once this happens they will never be completely smooth again. However, if you are desperately short of space, it is possible to store small quantities of material in polythene bags for a short period. To do this, you should place a dozen or so well pressed flowers on a sheet of blotting paper which must be cut slightly smaller than the bag, and then cover them with more blotting paper. Now slide flowers and blotting paper into the bag, press out the air and seal the top with adhesive tape. These bags of flowers can now be stored away under the pile of pressing books, or under the carpet, but take care when using the vacuum cleaner! (See page 33)

4 MAKING A START

As soon as your material is pressed and dry, the fun of making decorations can begin. ·

In addition to the flowers themselves, several other items will be required, but these will not be expensive. A beginner can usually start right away with a sheet of art paper, a paint brush, some adhesive and a picture frame. As more elaborate decorations are undertaken various other things will be necessary, but here again, these need not cost very much. One of the nice things about working with pressed flowers is that it is an *inexpensive* hobby, requiring only the simplest tools and equipment.

Below   *Some of the equipment needed when making pressed flower decorations*

The list below describes most pieces of equipment and their uses.

SOME THINGS YOU WILL NEED

Glue Use a brand with a latex or rubberized base, preferably one which remains usable for up to twenty minutes after being removed from the tube or jar (see list on page 6).

Art or **cartridge paper** or **thin card** This can be obtained from any good art shop or stationers. Choose white, cream, black or brown, but avoid beige or fawn coloured paper because the flowers will merge into them and be lost when they begin to fade.

Hair lacquer (hair spray) This is used to soften-up material which has become brittle through drying out too quickly. The flowers should be sprayed three or four times and allowed to dry out between each spraying. After the final spray they should be returned to the pressing books for 24 hours. Spraying with hair lacquer also helps to preserve the flower's colour.

Paints These should be poster paints and you will need the three basic primary colours, red, yellow and blue, plus black and white. By mixing any two of the primary colours you will have:

yellow + *blue* = *green*
red + *yellow* = *orange*
blue + *red* = *violet*

The addition of white to these six colours will give you *tints*, and by adding black you will get *shades*. The addition of black and white produces *tones* (see plate 1).

The use of paint should always be considered very carefully. The object of touching up a flower is to prolong its natural beauty rather than to improve on it.

Paint brushes You will need two or three fine brushes (size 0) to apply paint, and one thicker brush with a pointed end for moving the flowers into position and applying the glue. Buy good quality brushes, cheap ones have a nasty habit of shedding hairs over everything.

It is most important to keep the brushes clean. With poster paints a good wash in clean water is all that is needed. After cleaning, the brushes should be stood in a vase or jam-jar, *heads upwards* and left to dry.

Scissors You will require a pair of sharp scissors for cutting background paper, stalks etc.

Clear adhesive tape This should be approximately $\frac{5}{8}''$ (15 mm) wide and will be needed for binding and sealing edges.

Adhesive transparent film This can be obtained from most stationers, and is used to cover wall plaques, calendars, lampshades etc.

Trimmings Coloured adhesive tape or passe partout will be needed for some of the decorations described later in the book, and also some odd lengths of ribbon, cord and braid, but before you buy these it is well worth checking to see if there is not something in your sewing basket which will serve the purpose.

You will also need certain other essential equipment such as lampshades, picture frames and transparent finger plates, but these will be described in more detail in the following chapters.

It will be a great help if you can set aside a cupboard, or part of one, for the storage of your equipment, for it is surprising how much time is wasted when collecting tools from several places each time they are required.

TOUCHING UP

Like old soldiers, many pressed flowers would simply fade away if they were not touched up with a little poster paint.

Some purists object to the use of artificial colouring with pressed material, but I like to use it on early fading blooms and on white flowers, such as cow parsley and ox-eye daisies, which usually dry out a rather dingy cream. Provided the flowers are only lightly touched up, and the paint is matched as closely as possible to the blooms' natural colour, it can add a great deal to the decorative appeal of an arrangement. Flowers must never *look* painted, and one would not, for instance, paint a dainty quaking grass red, nor a lawn daisy blue. But it would be entirely appropriate if the filaments on a passion flower were lightly banded in purple, white and blue—as they are when the flower is growing. Paints should only be used to restore or prolong a flower's beauty, not to embellish it.

Here are some flowers which I consider benefit from a little discreet make-up:

Clover I like to highlight its centre whirl with a little white or dark green poster paint.

Cow parsley and Daisies these are touched up with white.

Alyssum saxatile, Cinquefoils and Wild parsnip these are painted with 'middle' yellow.

Heuchera I brush the tips of the tiny bell-like flowers lightly with crimson.

Roses all the small red roses I use in my decorations are painted with crimson to which I add a little black or white paint to give varying tints and shades (see plate 1).

Poster paints are much easier to use if they are first mixed with a drop of liquid detergent, and the lids of jam jars make excellent palettes as they can be washed quickly and take up very little storage space.

Flowers should always be touched up *before* they are stuck down in an arrangement, and all but clover, cow parsley and wild parsnip should be returned to the pressing book for a few hours as soon as they are dry. Petals are inclined to curl and become brittle after being painted so it is essential to press them flat again before they have a chance to crack or break off.

Any attractive material that has pressed well but shows signs of fading can be restored to its original colour by touching up. However, do not attempt to paint badly pressed or transparent flowers, they will only look garish and spoil the whole effect of your decoration.

STICKING DOWN

The most important thing to remember when you are sticking down your flowers is that the glue should be used *sparingly,* so that there is none leaking around stalks and grasses, and no blobs trapped under petals! Many pressed flower decorations are spoilt because the artist was too heavy-handed with the glue. So take care with sticking down, keep the adhesive away from the face of the flowers and clean off any surplus as you go along. Using a latex-based glue allows any smudges or mistakes to be removed easily with a clean rag or finger.

Start the sticking down operation by placing a small blob of adhesive on a saucer or in the lid of a jam jar. It will remain workable for quite a while, but as soon as it shows signs of drying out and becomes rubbery it should be wiped away and replaced with a fresh blob. Apply the adhesive to the flower, leaf or stem with the pointed end of a paint brush handle or cocktail stick. Simply dip the tip of the handle into the glue and then stroke it over the back of the leaf or stem.

To stick down a whole flower just put a tiny dab of adhesive on the centre back of the flower, then place the flower in position on the art paper and press down gently with your finger-tip. It is not necessary, except when you are using a plastic film covering, to glue every petal, the picture glass or finger plate cover will keep them flat and prevent them curling.

Single petals, such as delphinium and clematis, should have a spot of glue placed on the lower inside tip. There is no need to worry about the other end of the petal as the glass will hold it in place.

Page 38
Top left *Applying glue to the flower with the pointed end of a cocktail stick*
Top right *Stroking the glue along the centre back of a leaf*
Bottom left *Dabbing the glue onto the centre back of a flower*
Bottom right *Gluing the lower inside tip of a single petal*
Page 39
Top left *Stroking adhesive onto a stalk in two or three places*
Top right *Placing a dab of glue on stalk, tip, and either side of centre vein of a leaf*
Bottom left *Dabbing glue on each mimosa bobble*
Bottom right *Stroking glue along the stem and flower heads of grass*

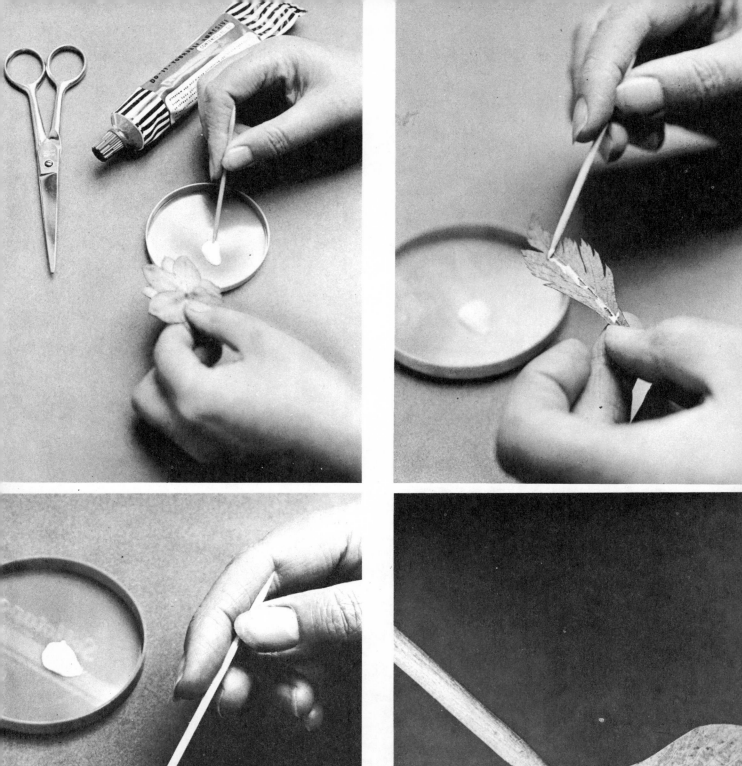
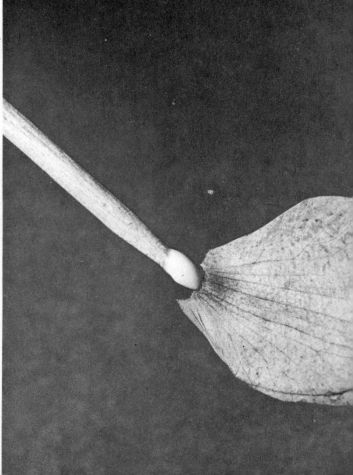
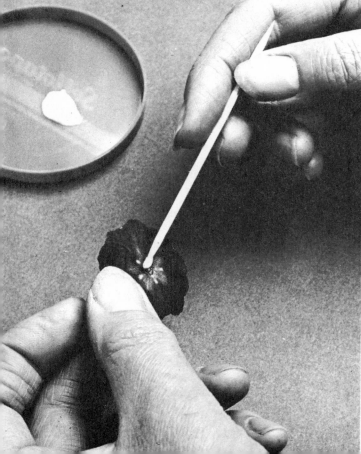

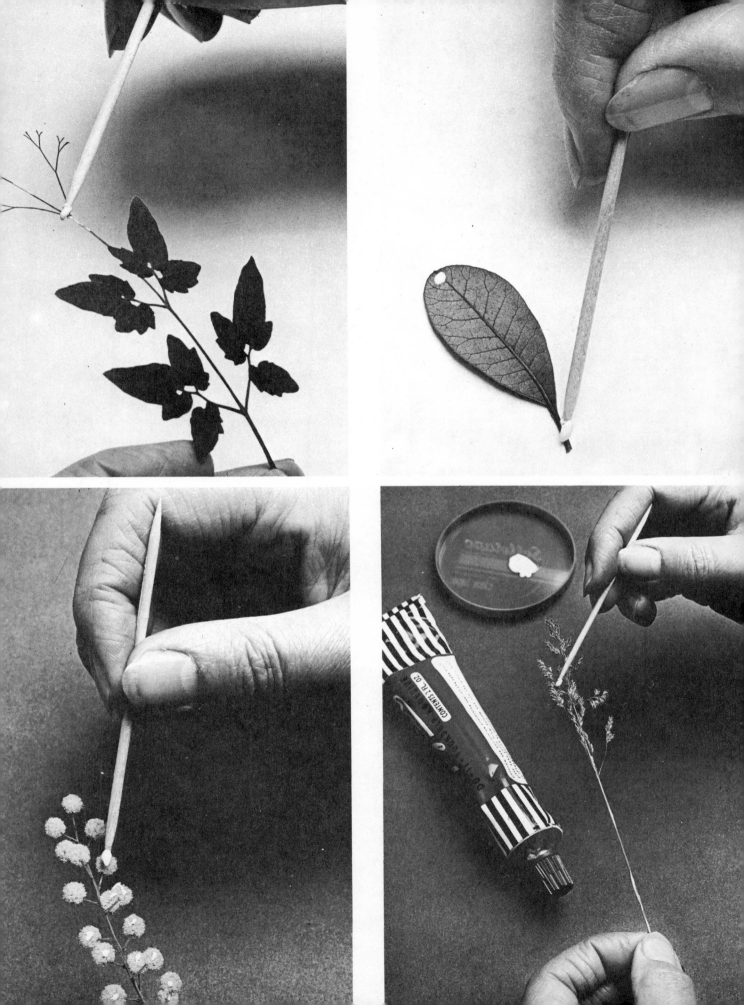

Stalks and tendrils just need a little adhesive stroked on in two or three places. It is not necessary to cover the whole stalk with glue, as long as it catches in one or two places when you press it down, it will stay in position.

To stick down leaves you should put a dab of glue on both the tip and the stalk end, and on either side of the middle vein, and with flowers such as mimosa and cow parsley, you should put the smallest possible dot of glue on each bobble or umbel. Be extra careful when you are sticking mimosa as the bobbles are fragile and fall off the main stalk if the decoration is knocked or shaken in any way.

Grasses should have a little adhesive stroked along the back of the stem in the same way as stalks and tendrils. You will also need a dab or two on the flower heads.

If you find you have stuck a flower down in the wrong position, it is best to pull it off petal by petal. Never try to remove the complete flower in one go in the hope that you can re-use it, because you may tear the background paper. Pull the flower off a little at a time and then rub the dried on glue off the paper with your finger-tip.

REMOVING POLLEN

Before framing or covering your pressed flowers all loose pollen, seeds and stamens should be carefully removed. This is best done by tapping the bottom edge of the decoration very gently on the table and then blowing off all the loosened bits and pieces. Buttercups and mimosa often shed a lot of pollen and this sticks to the inside of the glass or transparent covering and gives the decoration a dusty appearance. Specks of yellow pollen are particularly noticeable when the flowers are arranged on a black or dark-brown background, and unfortunately the picture glass or finger plate cover appears to magnify it.

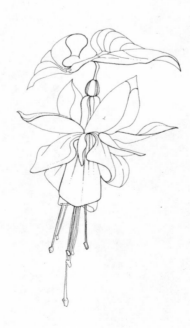

5 DESIGNING

Many beginners are nervous about designing, but there is really no need to be. Arranging pressed flowers is an art, so there can be few hard and fast rules. The designs you make with your flowers will depend entirely on you, for we are all individuals and so are our pressings. I can only guide you by pointing out the basic principles of good design and suggesting one or two outline ideas. Do not hesitate to experiment, and never reject an idea simply because you wonder if it would be acceptable to others. Since beauty is in the eye of the beholder you should use in your own home whatever type of arrangement appeals to you most. Let your creative powers have full play, and do not worry if, in the early days, the colours seem to clash and the shape goes a bit wrong. Your skill will soon grow and before very long you will be producing pressed flower decorations which will be real works of art.

WHAT MAKES A GOOD DESIGN

A good design must embrace three basic principles. These are scale, balance and harmony.

Scale is the relationship of length, breadth and height. This covers the size of the various components of an arrangement— flowers, foliage and stalks—and the size of the arrangement itself in relation to the background and the edging material or frame surrounding it.

Balance An arrangement must look well balanced and not lop-sided or top-heavy. Dark colours always appear heavier than light ones and textures, too, can influence balance. Smooth leaves and petals reflect light, while rough surfaced material tends to absorb it.

Harmony Colours and shapes must all harmonize into an attractive and satisfying whole. This is achieved by grading and blending colours and balancing and counter-balancing curves.

These, then, are the basic rules of good design, but do not feel that you have got to follow them, they are mainly guides for the beginner. As time goes on and you gain more experience you will find yourself developing your own particular style and bending, or even breaking, the rules to suit your arrangements.

STARTING A DESIGN

A design seldom just happens. It is usually the result of a well thought-out plan. Sometimes a flower, a curving stalk or a pair of well shaped leaves will give you an idea for an outline. Think about this line, the size of the arrangement and the colour scheme until you have a clear-cut picture in your mind's eye of what you want, and if you think it will help, try sketching it out roughly on a piece of paper. Now sort through your pressing books for flowers, leaves and grasses which will help emphasise the line. This is usually done with light coloured material and fine dainty things such as grasses, mimosa, cow parsley, small pointed leaves and tendrils. Next look for one, or perhaps two, special flowers to make a focal point from which the eye can range over the whole composition. Have confidence in yourself, know what you want to do and stick to it!

I find that I usually get my best ideas from the box of curving wisteria stalks which I keep on my work-table. With just two curved stalks I can make the four different outline designs shown on the next page.

the lazy S shape or Hogarth curve,
a heart shaped outline,
a C or crescent shape, which can be either left- or right-handed,
an open circle.

The beginner often fails to appreciate that flowers can be made to curve *inwards* as well as upwards, downwards and outwards. If flowers or leaves are made to curve in towards an open space in the centre of an arrangement (see illustration on plate 12) the space itself will become a focal point, and the whole design will look more restful and more subtly planned.

Space is very important in a design. Every flower, leaf, bud and stem must be seen clearly and to its best advantage. Newcomers to this hobby are often tempted to include all their most attractive pressings in one picture, and are then disappointed when the finished arrangement looks cluttered and overcrowded. So keep a tight rein on yourself! Remember that spaces can be as effective as flowers and aim for an airy, well balanced design.

I try to make all my arrangements look as if the flowers are still growing, because a stiff or formal design is very boring to look at over a long period. Usually, the quicker an arrangement is made, the more light-hearted and natural it will look. So, if the design has not come right after an hour or so, I cover it with blotting paper, weight it

Four outline designs

42

down and forget about it for three or four hours or even until the next day. Then, when I look at the arrangement again, the fault generally shows up immediately and I can put it right in a few minutes.

Another, and quicker, way of finding faults is to look at your arrangement through a hand mirror. Viewed from a different angle the mistake will often stand out like a sore thumb!

Every part of an arrangement must look exactly right. Each flower and leaf should fit in with its neighbour. Be a perfectionist, for the whole design can be ruined by just one odd stem leading nowhere, or by one flower too many. If a flower looks wrong when you are setting up the design, it will still look wrong when it is stuck down and the decoration is completed.

A NEAT BASE

In an oval, circular or vertical arrangement the base should be given a neat little design of its own to avoid a hard, sheared-off appearance. Small fronds of mimosa, tiny senecio greyii leaves, ivy leaves, eccremocarpus leaves and tendrils, quaking grass, rudbeckia, gaillardia and gazania petals will all make a pretty baseline and give the whole design a tidy and well finished look. Examples are shown on plates 4 and 5.

BACKGROUNDS

Some people use a fabric background such as silk or velvet with their pressed flowers, but I prefer to use thin card or blotting paper. Dried flowers can look most attractive when arranged on a background of material, but I do not like to see the more delicate pressed flowers on this type of backing. There is usually too great a contrast in texture, and this upsets the visual balance of the design so that the background appears to dominate the flowers. Both background and frame should always be secondary to the flowers so they must be chosen with care.

When deciding on a background colour remember to allow for the flowers fading over the years. It is no use arranging a design which includes ferns on a fawn background. In a few months the ferns will have faded to a golden brown and will disappear in a background of the same tone. Flowers like the celandine, which turns white after about a year, would also be lost if they were arranged on a white background. However, you can overcome this by placing the flower on a montana or prunus leaf to give it a nice dark background of its own.

For pictures, finger plates and firescreens I use black, white or cream backgrounds, but for smaller articles such as table mats and bookmarks I like to use crimson blotting paper.

Golden grasses, yellow, orange and white flowers, and all the silvery-grey leaves show up well on a black background, and silver and white leaves and flowers look lovely against a red or deep blue one.

A word of warning! Take extra care when you are removing blobs of glue, etc, from a blotting paper background as the hairy surface of the paper is very easily torn.

6 MAKING PICTURES AND FINGER PLATES

If you are new to the craft of making pressed flower decorations and are eager to try it, I suggest you start by making a picture. One about 10″ × 8″ (254 × 203 mm) is a good size, and if you do not have a design of your own in mind, a left-handed or right-handed C is a nice simple outline to begin with. It is also one of the quickest designs to execute so you will see the results almost at once and, even more important, it will not use up too many of your precious flowers!

If you are buying a picture frame, choose one with non-reflective or non-glare glass. This is essential if you intend using a dark background, because, with ordinary glass, all you are likely to see when you look at your picture from a distance is a reflection of the room.

PICTURES

As with all decorations, the first step in making a picture is to think about the design, the flowers you will use and their colours. Then, when you have a clear idea of what you want to do, you can select the most suitable background paper and cut it to fit the frame. To do this, you should lay the picture glass on the sheet of paper and draw around it with a pencil, then cut just inside the pencil line so that the paper is very slightly smaller than the glass.

Now look through your pressing books for a nicely curving stalk to form the outline of the design, and lay this in position on the background paper. You may have to cut bits from several different stalks to get the right curve, but any left-over pieces can be used up in another design (see page 46).

Next you should add the main flowers, perhaps a rose or a large delphinium with a few smaller flowers arranged around it.

Cut off any part of the stalk which is covered by the flowers as this would form a ridge under the petals and look unsightly.

Now look through your pressing books again, this time for some short curving stems and tendrils to break up the rather hard line of the main stalk. Take time to search for the right curve and for the best type of flower or leaf to put with it, for in all floral art the plant material is the main feature.

Move your flowers around on the background paper with a clean, dry paint brush, gently pushing them this way and that until they are correctly positioned, taking care to leave a good margin all round your arrangement so that it will not look cramped when it is framed.

Now add a few leaves, some mimosa fronds, sprigs of heather or heuchera, and three or four larkspur, tiny polyanthus or ursinia flowers to fill in and balance the design. The nice thing about the C shape is that it is so simple and effective, but because all flowers are different, no two crescent arrangements will ever be exactly the same.

When you are perfectly satisfied with your design, you can begin sticking it down. Leave the flowers just as they are on the art paper and carefully lift up the main stalk line with the brush end of your paint brush. Now dip the pointed end of another paint brush into a little adhesive and rub this underneath the stalk, then press it down with your fingers. Do the same with the main flowers and the smaller flowers around it, taking great care not to disturb the rest of the arrangement. Then lift, stick and press all the other flowers, leaves and stems in the same way.

Do remember to keep all windows and doors closed while you are arranging your flowers—a sudden draught could ruin everything! If you have to leave your work, even for a minute, cover it with blotting paper and place the picture glass on top.

I once spent many painstaking hours setting up a very large picture and all that was needed to complete the design before I started sticking it down, was one small raspberry leaf. This was in one of the pressing books which had overflowed into the dining-room. I was only away for a couple of minutes, but when I returned my arrangement had vanished and there, sitting in the middle of the work table, was Henry, our cat, patting paint brushes around and scattering flowers in all directions. I almost wept! So be warned, and make sure there are no draughts, no coughs or sneezes and no cats when you are designing.

Frame your picture as soon as it is finished. Pressed flower pictures should never be mounted as the flowers must be pressed right up against the glass to keep the petals from curling. Do ensure that there are no lumpy stalks or bulky centres as these will prevent the rest of the flowers from coming into contact with the glass. If necessary, pack the decoration against the glass with thick paper or a piece of cardboard. This picture is shown on plate 9.

Do not hang your picture in a damp room and do keep it well away from strong sunlight to prevent early fading. If one or two flowers should fade prematurely, these can easily be rubbed off with a clean finger and replaced with other flowers of a similar shape and size.

FINGER PLATES

There are two ways of making door finger plates. The flowers can either be arranged on a white or coloured background made of thin card, or they can be stuck down on a piece of transparent adhesive film so that

Left   *Drawing round the picture glass*

Right   *Cutting out the background paper*

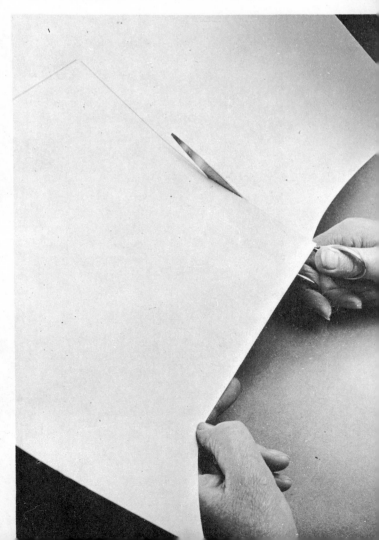

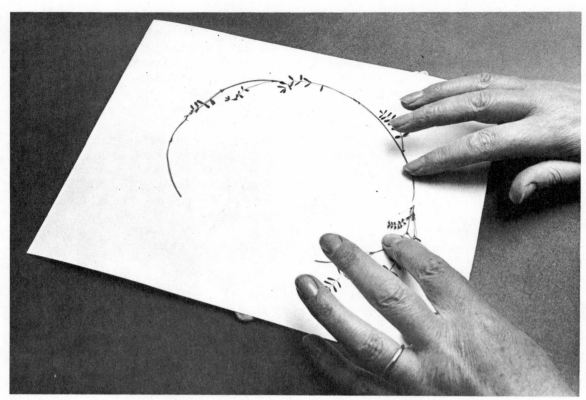

Above   *Positioning the outline stalks*   Below   *Adding the main flowers*

Above   *Filling in the details*

Below   *Sticking   down   the design*

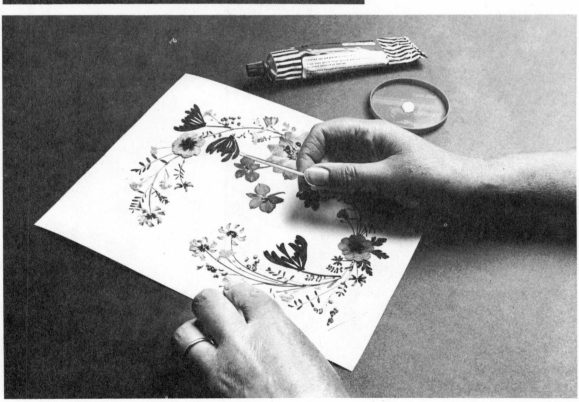

the door itself forms the background to the flowers.

If you are a beginner, I think you would be wise to make your first pair of finger plates with a card backing, then, if you do put a flower in the wrong place, it can be rubbed off. With an adhesive background, mistakes either have to be left for all to see, or everything must be scrapped and a fresh start made, because, once the flowers have come into contact with the plastic sheeting, there is no way of removing them without making a mess. Both types of finger plates can be made for just a few pence or well over a pound, depending on whether you cover your flowers with acrilic sheeting or glass. Ready-made panels measuring about 10″ × 2½″ (254 × 64 mm) can be bought from most hardware stores, or you can make your own from a sheet of double-glazing film. This can be cut with a pair of ordinary household scissors and has the advantage of allowing you to make your finger plates as long or as wide as you wish.

WITH A CARD BACKING

Materials :

A ready-made transparent glass or *acrilic finger plate* (or *cut your own from double-glazing film*)
A piece of thin card
Latex-based adhesive
Clear adhesive tape, approx : ½″ (13 mm) wide
Screws for fixing to the door

When you have decided on the background colour, lay the finger plate cover on the card and draw round it. Now cut inside the pencil line so that the piece of card is exactly the same size as the transparent cover.

Where space is limited, as it is in a finger plate, an arrangement which stresses the vertical line is usually the most effective. This is where some of those curving stalks I advised you to press, in Chapter 3, will come in useful.

To avoid the appearance of top-heaviness you should start your design by making a neat and compact base arrangement with

Plate 7
Top   *These wall plaques are made from house number-boards. I have used a light oak stain on the one with the Delphinium and Virginia creeper leaf and dark oak on the other one. The white flower is a Narcissus. I have touched it up with white poster paint as all but the centre had turned a dreary beige. I have also had to paint the Cineraria leaves as they turn dark green when they are lacquered and would have been lost on the dark background.*
Bottom   *This pretty glass-topped tray was a junk-shop find! Note the neat base arrangement and the way the flowers curve upwards and inwards.*

Plate 8
Five dark blue Delphinium flowers, golden brown Thalictrum leaves and a gently curving Wisteria stalk make up this simple but effective design for a lampshade. If you have no delphiniums, small red Roses, Polyanthus or Larkspur would be equally attractive substitutes.

Plate 9

Top   This is the picture described and shown on pages 44–7. The Alyssum saxatile has been lightly touched up with yellow poster paint. The Potentilla petals will fade but will turn a rich cream and will still look attractive because the dark centre retains its colour. The Honeysuckle buds were small enough to press in their entirety. They have been in the pressing book for three years and have changed from beige to this lovely rich brown.

Bottom   The three Passion flowers have false middles because the frame is shallow and their own centres would have prevented the glass from coming into contact with the other flowers. Resting on the silvery-grey undersides of the Raspberry leaves are three tiny autumn-tinted Berberis thunbergii leaves. The crimson Japanese maple leaves were picked up in a city park.

Plate 10

A group of smaller articles, some of which are particularly suitable for children to make.
Greetings card   Crimson blotting paper makes a cheerful background for Daisies, Horseshoe vetch, Cow parsley, Alyssum saxatile, Barley whiskers, Buttercup and Cineraria centuria leaflets. The daisies, cow parsley and alyssum saxatile have been touched up with a little poster paint.
Picture   A small, colourful arrangement using Roses, Larkspur, Eccremocarpus, Thalictrum and Quaking grass. The roses have been touched up with crimson poster paint.
Desk tidy   The pieces of Quaking grass used here are rather bulky and so they have formed tiny pockets in the transparent adhesive film. Smooth, flat leaves and flowers are best.
Bookmarks   The two backing materials are blotting paper and stiff art paper. Ribbon and transparent film are also suitable backgrounds for these simple arrangements.
Valentine   This lovely design uses Alyssum saxatile, Larkspur, Cow parsley, and Eccremocarpus.
Matchbox   The flowers and leaves show up well against the blue background. Again, the Barley whiskers are a little too thick and so have formed pockets in the covering.

three small ivy leaves, or a single lawn daisy and a few delphinium petals. Now add a stem of larkspur (buds and flowers), or a stem or two of montbretia or heuchera. Fill in the side spaces with such things as grasses, nipplewort, buttercups, clover, horseshoe vetch, ladies bedstraw, daisies and mimosa.

Leave a good margin all round the design and try to keep the arrangement nicely balanced. As space is so limited, stalks will play a big part in helping to guide the eye outwards and upwards. Designs for finger plates should be much more informal than those used in pictures and other large decorations, but this does not mean that the arrangement 'just happens'; the principles of good design must still be applied.

As soon as you are quite happy with your flowers, stick them down with adhesive in the way described for making pictures (see page 44). Now cover the design with the glass, acrilic sheeting, or double-glazing film, and bind the finger plate and the card together very firmly with clear adhesive tape. If you are using double-glazing film you will need to make a screw hole at each corner to fix the finger plate to the door.

If the finger plate is to be fixed to a sunny door, it is best to use non-fading or touched up material such as honeysuckle, clover, alyssum saxatile, cow parsley, daisies, wild parsnip and grasses, and to keep the design as uncluttered and simple as possible.

WITH A TRANSPARENT BACKING

Materials :
A ready-made transparent glass or acrilic finger plate
Transparent adhesive film
Screws for fixing to the door

Transparent adhesive film can be purchased from most stationers and decorators shops. There are several suitable brands, but do make sure that the material is really transparent, and that it is sufficiently sticky to hold fairly thick things like stalks and honeysuckle buds in place.

To begin, lay the finger plate cover on the

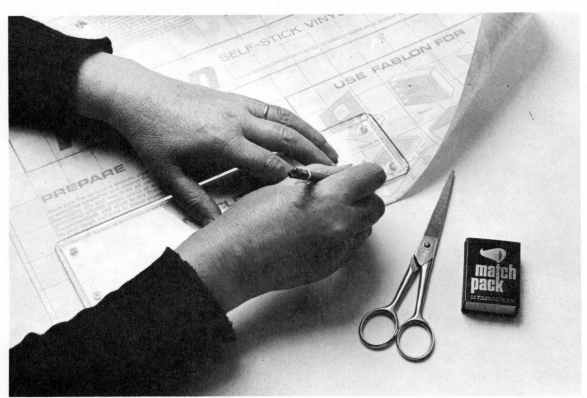

Above *Drawing round the finger plate on the paper backing*

Below *Marking the screw holes on the transparent film*

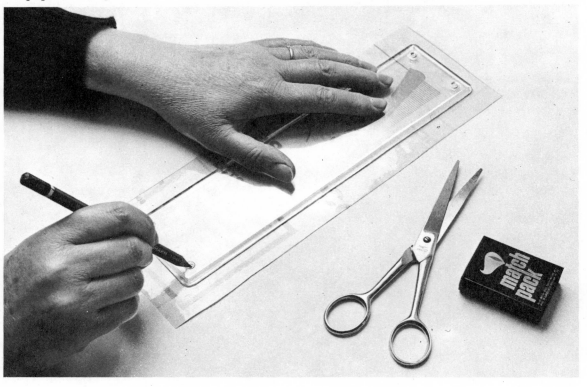

Above   *Arranging the flowers on the paper*
backing

Below   *Transferring the design to the trans-*
parent film

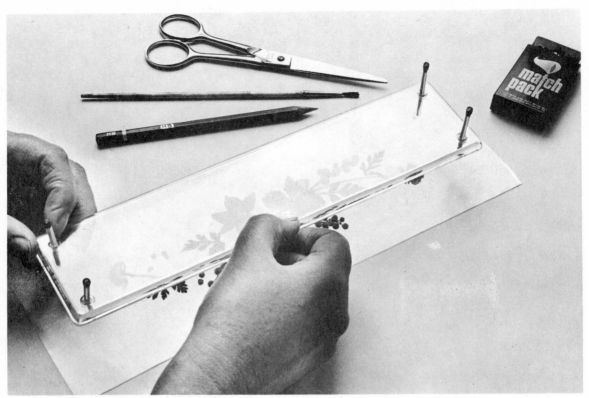

Above *Lining the matches up with the screw hole marks on the film*

Below *Sliding the finger plate down the matchsticks*

reverse side of the sheet of adhesive film and draw all round it. Now cut well outside the outline so that the piece of film is at least half an inch (13 mm) bigger all round than the finger plate.

Next, lay the finger plate on the *front* of the film and, with a thick pin or ball point pen, mark out the screw holes by pushing the pin through the holes in the fingerplate, until it makes a mark on the film.

Now lift a corner of the paper backing and peel it right off. Lay the piece of adhesive film on one side, and arrange your flowers on the paper backing, keeping the design well inside the pencilled outline of the finger plate. As soon as you are satisfied with your arrangement, transfer flowers, leaves and grasses, one at a time, on to the sticky side of the plastic film, pressing each one down firmly. When the whole design has been re-assembled on the piece of film go over it carefully to make certain every single stem and petal is well stuck down.

Now take the finger plate cover and insert a matchstick through each of the screw-holes, pushing them right through so that they are protruding by a $\frac{1}{4}$ inch (6 mm) or so. Place the cover over the flowers and line the matches up with the pin, or pen, marks on the plastic film, then slide the finger plate down the matchsticks until it rests on the film. Press down all round and remove the matches, then turn the whole thing over and roll a paint brush handle along the edges to seal them. To complete the finger plate, trim off all surplus adhesive film.

This may sound rather complicated, but with practice it all becomes quite automatic and you will be surprised to find how quickly you can make one of these floral finger plates.

7 SOME MORE THINGS TO MAKE

LIGHT SWITCH SURROUNDS

There will be no more grubby fingermarks around the light switch if you make one of these pretty pressed flower surrounds. They look most attractive against a plain wallpaper, especially when the light switch is near a door with a matching pressed flower finger plate.

Materials:
A ready-made transparent light switch sur-round (these can be purchased from most hardware stores)
A piece of thin card or thick drawing paper
Latex-based adhesive
Clear transparent tape, approx: ½" (13 mm) wide

Choose a suitable background colour then lay the surround on the card or art paper. Draw round the outside of the surround and then inside where the switch will be. Cut round the outside, then cut out the middle section.

As you will be designing in a very narrow space, you will have to rely on some grace-fully curving stems and tendrils to carry the arrangement around. Eccremocarpus tendrils, primrose or limnanthes stalks will all help to give the design this movement, and alyssum saxatile, daisies, buttercups and miniature roses could be grouped around them. Tiny ivy leaves, pieces of quaking grass or ladies bedstraw could also be included to fill in any obvious spaces.

When you have decided on the flowers to use, lay your design out on the art paper. Remember to nip off any bit of stalk which is covered by leaves or flowers, or the arrangement will be lumpy and the flowers will not be pressed up tightly against the cover.

As soon as you are fully satisfied with your arrangement, glue everything down. Then place the surround over the flowers and seal all the edges, inner and outer, with the adhesive tape.

The decoration is held in position on the wall by the light switch. If you are fixing the surround yourself, *do* remember to *turn off the current at the main switch* before you loosen the light switch cover.

WALL HANGINGS

These little Victorian tasselled pictures make delightful gifts and are soon snapped up at bazaars.

Materials:
A ready-made transparent glass or acrilic finger plate
A piece of card
Latex-based adhesive
Passe partout or coloured adhesive tape for framing
Cord or ribbon
Tassel (you can buy these ready-made, or you can make your own)
Small piece of thick paper for the back of the picture

Cut out the card and arrange the design on it as you did for the card-backed finger plate (page 48–9), but with this difference: leave a slightly larger margin all round to allow for framing with coloured adhesive tape or passe partout.

When you have stuck down your flowers, cover them with the finger plate and bind the edges firmly and evenly to the cardboard with the framing material. This is easier to do if you first hold them together in one or two places with small strips of trans-parent adhesive tape.

Now loop a cord or ribbon through the screw-holes at the top of the finger plate and fasten a matching tassel through the holes at the other end.

To neaten and finish off the back of the picture, cut another piece of card or a piece of thick wallpaper from one of your pressing books, and glue it on the back of the decoration so that it conceals the ends of the loop and tassel.

CALENDARS

Here is another pretty and useful way to display your flowers.

Materials :
A piece of cardboard
A piece of art or blotting paper
Latex-based adhesive
Transparent adhesive film
A short length of ribbon
Coloured adhesive tape or some other suitable edging material
A small calendar

Begin by cutting the cardboard to the required size (the calendar illustrated on plate 6 measures approximately 8″ × 11″ [203 × 279 mm]), then choose a suitable background colour and cut the art or blotting paper very slightly smaller than the cardboard. Now glue the art paper to the cardboard, taking care to see that it is perfectly smooth with no wrinkles or air bubbles.

Select your flowers and arrange your design, keeping it well away from the edges. Do not overcrowd your arrangement—let every leaf and petal stand out. Remember that a few curving stalks will loosen up the design and help the eye to rove over the whole arrangement.

When you are satisfied that each flower, leaf and bud is in its right place, stick them down with glue. Since you will be covering the design with adhesive film it is essential to stick down every single leaf and petal, because, once the film is in position, it is impossible for it to be removed to adjust anything without damaging all the flowers.

Covering with transparent adhesive film (See pages 56–7)

Cut the adhesive film about $1\frac{1}{2}$ inches (38 mm) larger all round than the decoration, then, with your finger nail, free the top edge and fold the protective backing paper back for about 2 inches (51 mm). Now, leaving about 1 inch (25 mm) overlap, place the sticky side of the film on the decoration and press down firmly. Smooth down with your hand, working from the centre to the edges, taking care not to trap any air bubbles. Hold a ruler on the stuck-down portion of film, and with the other hand grasp the freed edge of the backing paper and free another inch or so, then slide the ruler towards you. This pressure with the ruler will release the backing paper and make the film stick down. Continue in this way until the whole decoration is covered, then with your hand, or a soft cloth, smooth the film outwards from the centre to the edges.

This whole covering operation should be carried out as quickly as possible to avoid a build-up of static electricity, because this lifts stamens and any loose petals.

If you have not used this type of covering material before, try it out first on three or four odd flowers.

Having covered your calendar with plastic film, trim off the surplus and frame your arrangement with coloured adhesive tape. Now attach the small calendar to the bottom edge with a piece of ribbon. This can be fixed to the calendar with strips of adhesive tape or a dab of glue. Finally, make a small ribbon loop and attach this to the top of your calendar in the same way.

LAMPSHADES

An attractive and unusual way to display your flowers is on a lampshade. They will look very pretty in the daytime and at night, when the lamp is switched on, they will take on extra depth, rather like a 3-D picture, and look even more charming.

Colour is not so important when you are decorating lampshades. It is the design and the shape of the material which counts most. The arrangement should be kept as simple and uncluttered as possible and some well defined leaves and stems, such as herb Robert or Japanese maple, ladies bedstraw, goosegrass and broom should be included.

There are two ways of decorating a shade and the first method, using art paper is possibly the easiest, but, unfortunately, with this method the flowers do not show up quite so well when the lamp is switched on and so you lose some of the 3-D effect. However, if you are a beginner, I think it would be best to decorate your first lampshade in this way as it can sometimes be a little difficult to get the plastic covering film on smoothly with the second method.

First Method

Materials:
A plain lampshade
A piece of thin art paper
Latex-based adhesive
Transparent adhesive film (buy a non-yellowing brand)
Some quarter-inch braid
Some fringed braid

The shade can be any shape or size but it must be made of smooth, plain material. I like to see the flowers aranged on a white or pale cream shade, but you may feel differently. What matters most is that the flowers should show up well.

Begin by cutting a panel of art paper to the required size. If the shade is already trimmed with braid, cut the panel so that it fits in neatly between the top and bottom braid. If the shade is untrimmed, cut the panel very slightly narrower—about ¼-inch (6 mm)—than the depth of the shade.

Having done this, select and arrange your flowers, then glue them on to the paper

Below left *Placing the transparent film on the arrangement*

Below right *Sticking down the film with the aid of a ruler*

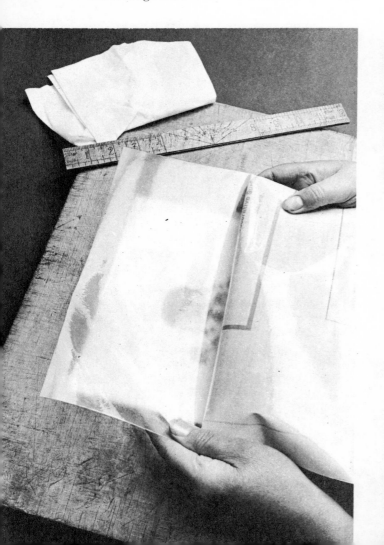

panel. Now cover your design with transparent film in the way described on page 55 and trim off the surplus. Spread adhesive thinly over the back of the panel then place it in position on the lampshade, smoothing it out from centre to edges and pressing it well down on to the shade.

The lampshade can now be trimmed. Glue the braid in place so that it covers the top of the panel and the top of the shade, then do the same at the bottom with the fringed braid. The sides of the floral panel can also be decorated with ¼-inch (6 mm) braid, and you can make another arrangement on the back of the shade so that it will look pretty from both angles.

Second method

In the second method the flowers are glued on to the lampshade itself. You should begin by arranging your flowers on

Below   *Smoothing out the film*

a piece of paper, then when you are quite happy with the design, the flowers can be stuck down on the shade. Transfer them one at a time, and stick them in the same order as they were arranged on the paper. Make sure every leaf and petal is stuck down firmly and remember to leave a good margin at the top and bottom of the shade. Do not make your design too big or the film may not be easy to stick down smoothly.

Now cut a piece of transparent adhesive film 1½ inches (38 mm) wider all round than the design, and pull back a little of the protective backing paper. Place the sticky side of the film over the flowers so that it overlaps the top of the arrangement by at least 1 inch (25 mm), and press down firmly. I find this operation is easier to carry out if the shade is fixed on to the lamp: it stops it from slipping. Now peel off a bit more of the backing paper and press the film down smoothly with your other hand. Continue in this way until all the flowers are covered, then cut off the surplus film at the top and bottom of the shade and press the edges down firmly. Some toning braid can now be glued around the lampshade. Note, if you have used a non-yellowing plastic film it will not be affected by the heat from the light bulb, but do make sure the bulb is the correct size for the shade.

TABLE MATS

Table mats are nice and easy to make, but remember they will be seen at close range, so use only your very best pressings. Take care too, when choosing the background colour. Pick one that will show off your flowers and blend happily with the other table appointments. Decorate them with daisies from your lawn or lovely autumn coloured leaves.

Materials:
A piece of glass, 24 oz or 32 oz cut to 6" × 6" (152 × 152 mm) or 7" × 7" (178 × 178 mm)
or
Piece of acrilic sheeting ⅛" (3 mm) thick cut to 6" × 6" (152 × 152 mm) or 7" × 7" (178 × 178 mm)

White or coloured art paper or *piece of thick cardboard* or *cork wall tile*
Veloured adhesive film or *some other suitable backing material if you are using cardboard*
Latex-based adhesive
Extra-strong adhesive tape

A glazier will cut the glass or acrilic sheeting for you. This thickness will take a fairly hot dinner plate but should not be used under an oven-hot dish.

Start by cutting the art paper, cardboard or cork tile (this can be cut with ordinary household scissors), to the same size as the glass. If you are using cardboard, you will also need to cut out a piece of veloured adhesive film and stick it to the back of the card. Now glue the art paper on to the cork or cardboard, taking care to see that it is perfectly smooth and very firmly stuck down.

Select your flowers and lay out the design, leaving a ½-inch (13 mm) margin all round. Senecio greyii leaves and buds show up well on a crimson or deep blue background, and buttercups, cow parsley and limnanthes look charming on a black or dark brown background.

Stick down your arrangement then cover it with the glass or acrilic sheet and bind glass and cardboard firmly together with extra-strong adhesive tape. You will find this is much easier to do if the edge of the mat overhangs the edge of the table by an inch or so.

Store your mats in a drawer or cupboard so that they will keep their colour for as long as possible.

TRAYS

A glass-topped tray will show off your flowers to advantage. You can make a new tray or give a new lease of life to an old one.

Materials :
Glass, 24 oz or 32 oz thick
Hardboard for backing
Sealer
Lacquer
Art paper
Clear adhesive tape

Have the glass and hardboard cut to the required size (the tray illustrated on plate 8 measures 12″ × 18″ [305 × 457 mm]), then paint the hardboard with a coat of sealer and two coats of lacquer.

Cut the art paper to the same size as the glass, then select your flowers and set out the design, remembering to leave a good margin all round.

Stick down all the flowers and cover them with the glass. Now bind the edges of the glass, art paper and hardboard firmly together with clear adhesive tape.

A picture framer will frame the tray for you and fix on a pair of handles if these are required.

If you are doing up an old tray, unscrew the feet, remove the back and slip out the old picture. Cut the background paper for your pressed flower design to exactly the same size as this picture, then arrange your flowers and stick them down. Now slide your decoration under the glass and replace the back of the tray. Before you screw the feet on again, make sure that the flowers are pressed right up against the glass to keep the petals from curling. To protect the flowers from spillages, fill in the space between the glass and the edge of the tray with any clear-drying glue which will adhere to glass.

FIRESCREENS

A firescreen decorated with holiday pressings makes a lovely souvenir of summer days (see plate 9).

You can sometimes pick up an old firescreen in a junk shop or you can do as I have done, and use a large picture frame and get someone to make two little wooden feet for it to stand on. However, if you do not have an old firescreen or suitable frame, you can easily make your own.

Materials :
A piece of 24 oz or 32 oz glass or *a piece of ⅛ inch (3 mm) acrilic sheet*
A piece of hardboard for backing
Sealer
Lacquer
Art paper

Extra-strong adhesive tape
Metallic edging tape

Have the glass and hardboard cut so that the finished firescreen will fit snugly into the fireplace. Paint the hardboard with a sealer and two coats of lacquer, then cut the art paper to the same size as the glass.

Select your flowers and make your design, leaving a good wide margin all round. As this will be a fairly large arrangement you will be able to use some of your bigger flowers, such as clematis and passion flower.

Stick down your design then bind glass, art paper and hardboard firmly together with extra-strong adhesive tape, and, if liked, the screen can be framed with a metallic edging tape.

Fit the screen into the fireplace and, if necessary, prop it up from behind with a couple of bricks.

VALENTINES

Love is never out of fashion; only the manner of the declaration changes. In great grand-mama's time, tokens of love were more lavish, and young girls would wait anxiously for the arrival of enchanting, lacy cards bearing tender messages on flowered backgrounds. The flowers themselves would also carry a message, and some of their meanings still hold good today.

Why not send your loved one a beautiful handmade Valentine? The following list will help you to choose the right floral message.

Alyssum *sweet*
Ash *grandeur*
Anemone *forsaken*
Aspen *lamentation*
Bramble *remorse*
Broom *humility*
Celandine *joys to come*
Christmas rose *relieve my anxiety*
Cinquefoil *maternal affection*
Clematis *mental beauty*
Clover (four-leaved) *be mine*
Clover (white) *think of me*
Daffodil *regard*

Daisy (white, garden) *I will*
Daisy (wild) *innocence*
Fennel *strength of mind*
Fern *fascination or sincerity*
Fuchsia *amiability*
Honeysuckle *truthfulness*
Hydrangea *heartlessness*
Ivy *friendship or marriage*
Larkspur *read my heart*
Lavender *distrust*
London pride *frivolity*
Mountain ash *prudence*
Oak *hospitality*
Pansy *ever in my thoughts*
Passion flower *religious superstition*
Polyanthus (crimson) *the heart's mystery*
Rose *love*
Rose (deep red) *bashful love*
Rudbeckia *justice*
Sycamore *curiosity*
Tulip (red) *declaration of love*
Tulip (yellow) *hopeless love*
Wheat *riches*
Willow *weeping*

To make a Valentine similar to the one in the picture you will need:

Four white paper doilies with a lacy design
A small piece of crimson blotting paper
Latex-based adhesive
Transparent adhesive film
Coloured embroidery silk

Cut a small red heart shape from the blotting paper and glue into position on the smooth, centre circle of one of the doilies. Now sort through your flowers and leaves and take out those which are most suitable for size, shape, colour and meaning. Make your arrangement and stick everything well down on the centre of the doily, then cut a piece of adhesive film to the exact size of the centre circle and peel off the backing paper. Gently press the film down over the heart and flowers and smooth out carefully.

Finally, to strengthen the valentine, thread a needle with coloured silk and sew all four doilies together, stitching through the holes in the lace to form an attractive pattern.

FLOWERS LACQUERED TO WOOD

Pressed flowers can be protected and held in place with transparent lacquer, so if you have any wooden articles which need brightening up, why not try decorating them with some of your pressings? Old wooden trays, bookends or cigarette boxes are all quite easy to decorate, or you can buy a piece of nicely grained wood and make an attractive wall plaque.

Make sure that you buy a lacquer which is quite clear and water-proof when dry. If you are buying wood to decorate, choose a piece with a fairly plain, but pleasing, surface. Do not buy anything with a grain which might detract from the flowers.

Start by rubbing down the wood with fine sandpaper. When it is perfectly smooth, remove every speck of dust from the surface and apply a thin coating of lacquer, then let it dry. If you are using a brush to apply the lacquer, you can stop the hairs from hardening by standing them in a tin of lacquer remover. When the first coat of lacquer is completely dry, apply a second coat and arrange your flowers in a pretty design on the wet surface, pressing them down gently with a brush so that they will stay in position. When this second coat of lacquer is thoroughly dry, cover flowers and wood with yet another coat. Flowers with thick stems or middles absorb a lot of lacquer, so these must have extra coats until the lacquer dries on the surface and they are completely covered, otherwise they may lift or rub off.

Do ensure that the lacquer is dry before you apply another coat. Although it takes time to apply all these layers, it is well worth doing as it makes the decoration much easier to keep clean. If you are using new wood or a piece of thin board, lacquer the back of the decoration as well to prevent it warping.

8 GIFTS FOR CHILDREN TO MAKE

With a little guidance, children can derive much pleasure from pressing their own flowers and making them into pretty and useful Christmas or birthday presents for relatives and friends.

Give them a pressing book of their own and show them which are the best flowers and leaves to press. Buttercups, daisies, heather, heuchera, red primula polyanthus, grasses and herb Robert leaves are all suitable for decorating small objects, and they also keep their colour fairly well and are easy to press.

It is a good idea to keep one or two extra-large matchboxes and a few disposable cups and plates in the house, then, on one of those miserable wet days when the children have nothing to occupy them, you will be able to introduce them to the fascinating craft of making pressed flower decorations.

The gifts described below are all quick and easy to make, and are sure to delight the recipients, for few things give more pleasure than a present that a child has taken time and trouble to make.

GREETINGS CARDS

Materials:
Cardboard photo mounts or *blank cards*
Cartridge paper
Latex-based adhesive
Transparent adhesive film.

If you are using a photo mount, you will need to cut a piece of art or cartridge paper very slightly larger all round than the inner frame. Having done this, choose your flowers and lay out your design. When you are quite happy with your arrangement,

stick the flowers on to the paper with the adhesive, making sure that every leaf and petal is well stuck down. Now cut off a piece of adhesive film. To be on the safe side, this should be about 1 inch (25 mm) larger all round than the picture. Free a corner of the film with a finger nail and pull off the backing paper, then, leaving 1 inch (25 mm) overlap, place the sticky side of the film over the picture and smooth it down carefully with your hand, working from the centre out towards the edges (see page 55). Cut off the surplus film and slip the picture inside the photo mount, then write an appropriate greeting on the bottom of the card. Later, the picture can be taken out of the cardboard mount and put in a proper frame.

Blank cards can be bought from most good stationers, or you can make your own from cartridge paper. Start by arranging your flowers on the front of the card and sticking them down in the usual way. When everything is well stuck down, cover the arrangement with plastic film. This should be cut a bit wider and longer than the card, and must be pressed down firmly at the edges before trimming off the surplus.

If you want to write a message on the front of the card, you must do it on the card before you cover it with transparent film.

MATCHBOXES

Materials:
A large matchbox
A piece of stiff art paper or *thin card*
Latex-based adhesive
Transparent adhesive film
Coloured adhesive tape

Cut a piece of art paper to the exact size of the matchbox and stick it on to the box with adhesive. Choose a few small flowers and leaves and make a pretty arrangement, then glue them in position. Now cut a piece of adhesive film a little larger than the matchbox, peel off the backing paper, and press it down quickly and carefully over the flowers. Trim off the excess covering and decorate each end of the matchbox with a strip of coloured adhesive tape, cut with pinking shears.

WALL PLAQUES

Materials:
A plain 7″ (178 mm) or 7½″ (191 mm) disposable plate
Latex-based adhesive
Transparent adhesive film
Coloured braid or some other suitable edging material
Small piece of adhesive putty or *Plasticene*

Choose some flowers from your pressing book and make an attractive design with them in the centre of the plate. Stick them all down with the adhesive, then cut a piece of plastic film to the same size as the centre of the plate. Remove the backing paper and press the sticky side of the film on to your flowers. Take care not to trap any air bubbles and make sure it is well stuck down all round the edge. Now make an inner circular frame for your arrangement with some pretty braid or ribbon, and glue in place.

To hang your plaque, pull off a little bit of adhesive putty or Plasticene and roll it into a ball. Place the ball on the centre back of the plate, then press the plate to the wall and it will stay up. It will not mark the wall, but if you have to take it down again, do pull it off very carefully so that it does not tear the wallpaper.

Below   *Martin covering a greetings card with transparent film*

BOOKMARKS

Materials:
A short length of 1 inch (25 mm) ribbon
Art or *cartridge* or *blotting paper*
A piece of transparent adhesive film
Latex-based adhesive
Embroidery silks
A pair of pinking shears.

Bookmarks can be made with a ribbon backing, a paper backing or a transparent backing, and as the flowers will spend most of their time in a closed book, away from the light, you will also have a wide choice of material. Many poor pressers such as primroses and celandines, can be used to decorate a bookmark, but do not use any bulky flowers as a thick marker could damage the book. Two examples of bookmarks are illustrated on plate 10.

With ribbon backing

To make a marker with a ribbon backing you will need a piece of ribbon 1 inch (25 mm) wide by 8 inches (203 mm) long. Choose your flowers and arrange them on the ribbon. As the design will have to fit into a very narrow space you will find that long slender grasses, single flower petals and leaf segments are especially useful. Glue your flowers on to the ribbon with a tiny dab of adhesive, then cut off two pieces of adhesive film a bit larger all round than the ribbon. Cover your design with one piece of film and cover the back of the ribbon with the second piece. Trim off the surplus film and neaten the ends of the bookmark by cutting them into a V shape or trimming them with pinking shears.

With paper backing

This marker is made in the same way, but the paper should be cut about 1 inch (25 mm) shorter. After covering the back and front of the marker with adhesive film, trim the ends with a small tassel made from embroidery silk or a piece of narrow ribbon.

With transparent backing

Cut two pieces of transparent adhesive film 2″ × 9″ (51 mm × 229 mm). Select your flowers and make your design on a 1″ × 8″ (25 mm × 203 mm) strip of scrap paper. Remove the backing paper from one of the lengths of plastic and place the film on the table, sticky side up. Now transfer your design on to the adhesive film. Press each flower and leaf down firmly, then remove the backing from the second piece of film and cover the flowers with it in the usual way. Trim back the surplus film until the finished bookmark measures approximately 1″ × 8″ (25 mm × 203 mm), then oversew the edges with coloured silk and fix a matching tassel at each end.

DESK TIDY OR PENCIL HOLDER

Materials:
A plain white, red or blue disposable cup
A tiny piece of veloured adhesive film or *thin card*
Small lump of adhesive putty or *Plasticene*
Latex-based adhesive
A piece of transparent adhesive film
A short length of narrow braid

To prevent the cup toppling over when it is filled with pens and pencils, you must first weight the base. To do this, you should cut a circle of veloured adhesive film or thin card to the exact size of the base of the cup. Now turn the cup upside down and press a lump of adhesive putty into the base so that it fills the hollow almost to the rim. Make sure it is perfectly smooth and level, then press on the adhesive film or cardboard circle.

Select some pretty leaves and grasses and glue them on to the cup with the adhesive, keeping your design quite small. Now cut a piece of transparent film just a little larger than your design. Peel off the backing and press the sticky side down over your arrangement. Smooth it out carefully and trim off the surplus at the top and bottom. Finish by gluing some pretty braid under the rim at the top of the pencil holder (see illustration overleaf and on plate 10).

PRESSED FLOWER PRINTS

Many flowers and leaves can be used as stamps for printing. They will not be strong enough to print dozens of copies, but if they are handled carefully, each flower or leaf should make eight or nine prints to decorate greeting cards or stationery.

Use either poster paint or ink, and make a few test prints first with the flower or leaf you intend using to find out just how much paint or ink you will need to apply for the best results.

Start by painting an even coat of ink on one side of the leaf with a paint brush, then turn the leaf over and place the inked side on the card or paper you want to decorate. Cover the leaf with a piece of blotting paper then, using the palm of your hand or a roll of absorbent tissue, smooth over blotting paper and leaf with firm, even strokes. Now remove the blotting paper and lift off the leaf, taking care not to smudge it. If

Below   Weighting the base of the desk tidy

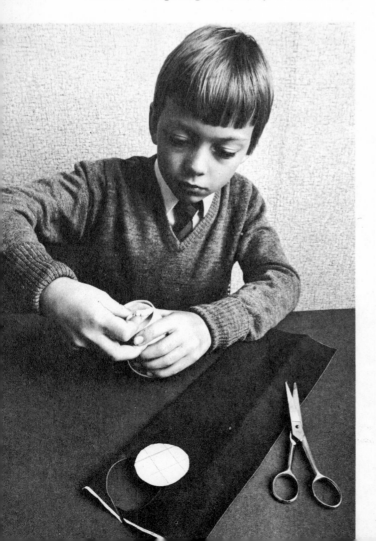

some parts have not printed as well as others, lightly paint in the faint parts with a fine paint brush. *Do not* attempt to re-ink the leaf and place it over the design again, it will only result in a blurred double image as it is almost impossible to put the leaf down again in exactly the same position. When you have printed your motif, leave the paper on one side to dry for a few hours before using or storing it.

You can print on most types of paper, but to be on the safe side, do a few test prints first as different papers produce different effects. If you use flowers and leaves with interesting outlines and prominent veins or other markings, you will find that your designs stand out better and look more attractive.

Plate 11
Top left   *Sycamore leaves, Herb Robert leaves and Daisies make good stamps for printing. This shows first and sixth printing with these leaves and flowers. Unfortunately, one of the herb Robert leaves disintegrated after the third print.*
Top right   *See how bold Daisies become when they are placed on a crimson background. Both daisies and Cow parsley have been touched up with white poster paint.*
Bottom   *The blue, orange and brown tones of this picture were inspired by a wallpaper design in one of the pressing books. The Mimosa will turn a burnt orange colour after about a year and will then balance the stronger colour of the Larkspur.*

Plate 12
Top left   *The lady with a parasol is very proud of her fashionable Clematis and Delphinium gown. Other flowers used are Cow parsley, Statice, Allysum saxatile, Thalictrum, Silverweed, Weigela, Buttercup, Rose, Mimosa, Japanese maple and Mallow. A full description of her outfit can be found on page 69.*
Top right   *Floraltails make good messengers and are easily made from bits and pieces. These little birds are described more fully on page 67.*
Bottom   *There are sixteen different kinds of pressed flowers in this light and airy arrangement. The white leaves and flowers look cool and refreshing, and the dark open space in the centre adds to the tranquil impression. This picture is referred to on page 42.*

Gift-bearing Floraltails

Get well soon

A. Barred Willow-tail
B. Spotted Silverweed
C. Yellow-eyed Ribwort
D. Fennel Warbler

9 PRESSED FLOWER CARTOONS

Now we come to an entirely different sort of pressed flower decoration—the collage cartoon. Of all the hundreds of decorations I have made, my first cartoon picture is the one which has given me most pleasure and satisfaction. It took far less time to make than an ordinary flower picture, and I was particularly pleased to discover that although I am quite hopeless at drawing I could make leafy animals and flower-petal people very easily indeed. In fact most of these cartoon figures are ready-made for you—it is simply a matter of finding the right pieces and sticking them down in the right positions, rather like doing a jig-saw puzzle. On pages 73–4 I have made a list of some useful 'pieces' so that you will know what to look for when you start making your own cartoons.

Once you have got used to the idea of leaves and flowers playing dual roles, you will begin to see possibilities in many plants which earlier you would have considered quite unsuitable for a pressed flower decoration. Take a clematis tangutica seed-head, or a piece of old-man's-beard for example. They would look quite out of place in a finger plate or flower picture, but they are ideal for cartoons if you want your little people to have a good head of hair, although a trifle unruly.

As you develop a more imaginative eye you will notice that many flowers resemble heads and bodies, and that honeysuckle buds look like arms and legs. Incidentally, you would be wise to press a good stock of these buds because your cartoon characters will need arms to wave and legs to run about on. By changing the angle of the buds you can make your fingers run, walk, dance, stand up or fall down in a moment, and you will not have to draw anything!

If you look at some meadow buttercups, you will see that their leaves make excellent hands with long, tapering fingers and their tight little buds will make noses. Study a senecio cineraria leaf and you will notice that each leaf section has a ready-made left or right gloved hand, or little grey paws for a mouse. Grasses, too, can lead a double life. In cartoons they become trees and bushes, and their long stalks make pavements or distant horizons.

In autumn, when the parks and roadsides are carpeted with leaves, you will be able to gather up hundreds of grounded 'birds'. All they will need is a wipe with a damp cloth and after a week or two in the pressing books they will ready for you to make into 'Floraltails', those most helpful—and versatile—birds you see on page 66 and plate 12.

My first Floraltail was made quite by accident. I was setting out an arrangement for a firescreen when my sleeve caught the edge of the design and pushed some of the leaves out of position. As I was putting them all back again I noticed that one small bramble leaf had got a 'tail' of silverweed which made it look like some exotic bird, I immediately forgot all about the firescreen and started looking through my pressing books for a 'wing' and an 'eye' and some 'feet', and in just a few minutes my very first Floraltail was born. Since then dozens more have emerged from the pressing books. Besides the gift-bearing species you see on plate 12, and the Apologetic Floraltail overleaf there are Congratulatory Floraltails who wave flags cut from contrasting paper, and the latest 'hatch' produced a fine flock of Banner-bearing Floraltails which were sent flying off to announce the arrival of a friend's baby daughter.

Unlike a design for a pressed flower picture which requires both thought and time, a cartoon collage usually just happens. You will see a certain flower or leaf as I did with my Floraltails, and suddenly an idea is born and you will be hurriedly searching through your pressings for the right bits and pieces to complete your cartoon.

I try not to cut anything with scissors for much of the fun is in hunting for a leaf or bud that is not only the right shape, but the right size too! But I must admit that I do sometimes cheat a little by folding or bending a leaf just before it goes into the pressing book. I did this with the sumach leaflets I used for the man's sleeves and trousers in the *Going for a walk* cartoon on page 72, but there was no cheating with his head; the nose and mouth were cut out by a hungry caterpillar!

Try not to be in too much of a hurry to stick down your cartoon. It is best to cover it with a sheet of glass and leave it unstuck for a few days. Look at it every once in a while, then, if you see a mistake or change your mind about the position of a leg or an arm, you can alter the design without any trouble.

Try to keep your cartoons as neat and simple as possible. If you add too many fussy details, your collages will look cluttered, like a woman wearing too much jewellery on a flowered dress.

Keep your work spotlessly clean and, when framing your cartoon, make sure that every leaf and petal is pressed right up against the glass. Finally, and most important, enjoy yourself!

On the following pages there are some examples to give you ideas for your own cartoons.

FLORALTAILS

These little birds are made from odd leaves and left overs! They are quick and easy to make, and a good way of using up all those bits and pieces which are usually lying around after you have designed a picture or finger plate (see opposite and on plate 12).

Each bird is carrying a little gift. The *Barred Willowtail* has a bouquet of flowers and a get-well-soon note, the *Spotted Silverweed* has a bunch of grapes, the *Yellow-eyed Ribwort* has four bananas and the rather anxious-looking *Fennel Warbler* has a large potted plant.

HELP!

This frightened lady needs no face, her anthemis daisy hair, outstretched senecio cineraria hands and hurrying honeysuckle legs are all that is necessary to express her horror of 'creepy-crawlies'. What a blessing she is wearing her wide daffodil trumpet skirt! A narrow senecio greyii or prunus leaf skirt would have slowed her down considerably.

The large spider is made from clematis montana. Two oval-shaped leaves form the body and the little end leaves make four of his legs, his other legs and feelers are made from tiny pieces of montana stalk. The angry winged creature is made from a montbretia bud and a sycamore seed pod. His antennae are more pieces of montana stalk and his sting is a bit off a buttercup leaf.

"TAXI!"

The smart lady hailing the taxi is wearing a beautifully tailored bramble leaf costume with a delphinium petal collar held in place by a mimosa brooch. On her polyanthus head she wears a little potentilla calyx hat trimmed with statice. Her arms are honeysuckle buds and in one of her sycamore leaf hands she carries a rose petal bag with a statice flower handle, and a clematis montana leaf umbrella. Her legs and dainty high-heeled shoes are also made from clematis montana, but this time I have used the very tiny end leaves.

Mrs Poly's son has a clover head and a Virginia creeper leaf body. His arms and legs are honeysuckle buds and his smart yellow tie is an anthemis daisy petal. In his montana leaf hand he holds a 'whirly' toy made from a buttercup bud.

His sister is sporting a larkspur bud cap on her pretty potentilla head. The top half of her dress is made from a purple cow parsley leaf, trimmed with white florets, and her skirt is part of a daffodil. If you look closely, you will see that I have had to give her an underskirt (another piece of daffodil) because she was showing a little too much of her montana legs! Her scarf is made from two tiny pieces of leaf and, like the rest of her family, her arms are made from honeysuckle buds. Two very young eccremocarpus leaves were used for her hands and her bag is a delphinium petal with a mimosa bobble clasp.

68

LADY WITH A PARASOL

This type of collage gives you a chance to do a spot of dress designing! Turn the pages of your pressing books and there, waiting to be made into crinolines and trouser-suits, mini-skirts and fur-trimmed coats, are both plain and patterned materials in a wide range of colours from sober greys and browns to dashing reds and yellows.

The lady in this picture wears a gown of clematis and delphinium petals sprigged with cow parsley, statice, alyssum saxatile and tiny yellow thalicyrum leaves. Her cape is made from silverweed and purple cow parsley leaves, and her bonnet is a delphinium flower. Her weigela bud sleeve has a purple statice cuff and her slender fingers are buttercup leaves. In one hand she carries a smart rose petal reticule fastened with a mimosa bobble and in the other, a pretty lace-trimmed parasol made from a japanese maple leaf, four common mallow petals and four cow parsley florets. Unfortunately, I have glued the maple leaf a little too far from the lady's head, but I decided to leave it there as it was the only maple leaf I had at the time and I thought its colour went rather well with the rest of her outfit. We must therefore suppose she has raised her parasol on high to show off her handsome clematis seed hair!

This cartoon is shown in colour on plate 12.

"YOUNG BIRDS HAVE NO MANNERS THESE DAYS!"

This cartoon measures 10″ × 8″ (254 mm × 203 mm) and is one of the easiest to make. The body of the elderly bird on the left of the picture was made by placing a clematis montana leaf over all but a quarter of a Virginia creeper leaflet. The montana leaf forms the wings and the back, and a few bits of silverweed have been added to represent feathers. Her neck and bill are also made from Virginia creeper and her head is an anthemis daisy centre. (An ox-eye daisy would have done just as well). The feathers round her head are more bits of silverweed, and her eye is a lupin seed with a blob of white poster paint. Her long legs are pieces of goosegrass and her feet are tiny turkey oak leaves with a bit of the stalk attached.

Her friend was made in the same way, but two mountain ash leaflets were used for his body and a cow parsley leaf, which had been folded over at the time of pressing, was used to make his neck. The duck has a senecio greyii body with herb Robert wings and a silverweed neck. His feet are pieces of rudbeckia petal and his head is a honey-suckle leaf with a weigela bud for the bill. His eager eye was made by painting a quaking grass spikelet with poster paint and adding two little bits of silverweed, and the worm he is about to gobble is a thick, twirly piece of eccremocarpus. Note the slanting angle of the stalks and grasses, these help to indicate speed and excitement.

"Young birds have no manners these days"   W. G. Spencer 1973

70

DOWN IN THE DEEP BLUE SEA

The deep blue sea is a piece of art card 8″ × 6″ (203 mm × 152 mm). Six anthemis daisy petals and four bermuda grass heads make the shoals of smaller fish. The large fish on the left has a cotinus leaf for its body and pieces of raspberry leaf form its fins and tail. A small clary leaf and a lupin seed make its beady eye and its mouth is a horseshoe vetch floret. The other large fish on the right of the picture is made from a senecio greyii leaf. A tiny eccremocarpus leaf was used for the mouth and the fins are made from three Virginia creeper leaflets and a piece of turkey oak leaf. Its tail is made from two poppy petals and the scales are potentilla petals. The four other fish are also made from senecio greyii leaves and their tails are the end bracts of clary. Their fins are horseshoe vetch and silver-weed, and muscari seeds make their eyes. The sea-urchin in the bottom left-hand corner is a clover head and the star-fish is made from five horseshoe vetch florets. The bubbles are quaking grass and this together with ladies' bedstraw, fennel, barren brome grass and other bits of grass make up the plant life.

GOING FOR A WALK

I have already mentioned on page 66 that a hungry caterpillar nibbled the man's head for me and how I folded the six sumach leaves I have used for his arms and legs. The lower half of his body and his hat and tie are also made from sumach leaves. I found three of these leaves lying on the floor behind a pile of pressing books. They must have been there for some time, because they were very dry and brittle and as soon as I touched them they broke into pieces. However, after a few sprays with hair lacquer I was able to trim them into shape with my thumb nail and use them in this cartoon. Bits of senecio cineraria leaf make his gloved hands and his shoes are made from an empty broom seedpod. The walking stick is a piece of goosegrass stem and its handle is a fuchsia seed-box.

The little dog was made from a number of bits and pieces. Its tail is part of a willow leaf and its body is a small folded prunus leaf. Honeysuckle buds make its scampering legs, and its ruff and the man's few hairs are made from a clematis seed-head.

USEFUL ODDMENTS

Here is a list of some useful floral bits and pieces for your cartoons.

MEN, WOMEN AND CHILDREN

Heads Anthemis daisy, lawn daisy, ox-eye daisy, clover, rounded cotinus leaf, red primula polyanthus, deep mauve primula auricula, inner seed cases of honesty, buttercup.

Bodies Goosegrass, senecio greyii leaf, bramble leaflet, sumach leaves, mountain ash leaves, clover leaf, small oak leaf, any small autumn-tinted leaf, anemone petal, single Virginia creeper leaflet.

Arms and legs Honeysuckle buds, small folded sumach leaf, large anthemis daisy petals, goosegrass leaflet, willow leaves, montbretia buds.

Hands Buttercup leaves, part of a senecio cinerarea leaf, tiny pointed eccremocarpus leaf, very young end leaves of sycamore.

Feet Broom buds, laburnum buds and lupin seed pods, end shoots of clematis montana, honeysuckle buds, montbretia buds, passion flower stamens.

Hair Clematis tangutica seed head, pasque flower seed head, old-man's-beard, squirrel tail grass.

Nose Buttercup bud, senecio greyii bud, pointed end of a petal or leaf.

Eyes Tiny senecio greyii leaves, orange cotoneaster leaves, broom seeds, muscari seeds, buttercup bud, quaking grass (or paint in the eye on a tiny circle of white paper).

SOME SMART CLOTHES AND ACCESSORIES

Dresses One tulip petal, bramble leaf, oak leaf, one large clematis petal, delphinium petals, three clematis petals for crinolines, half a small daffodil trumpet for a short skirt, half a large daffodil trumpet for a longer skirt, two herb Robert leaves for a ballet skirt, ash leaves, two thick goose-grass leaflets for a blouse and skirt, anemone petal.

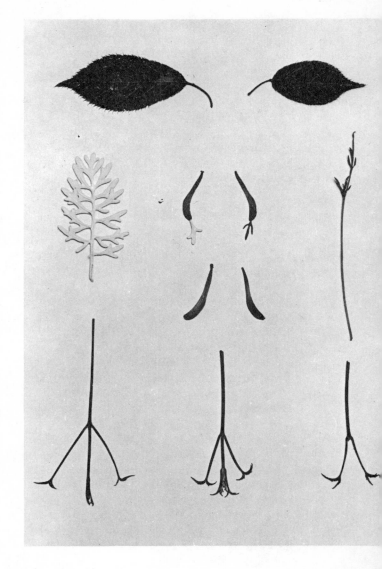

Above *To change a leaf such as the two above into a bird, snip off the stalk, add a bit of Quaking grass or a Mimosa bobble for an eye, the end of a Raspberry leaf for a wing, Buttercup side-leaves for feet, and two slim leaves or petals for a tail. For ladies' legs and shoes, snip off the young end-shoots of Clematis montana. When they are pressed and dry, remove the middle stem (bottom right above) and you have a pair of slim legs and smart shoes. Honeysuckle buds make stouter legs, and also arms and shoulders. For hands, use side-leaves from a buttercup or one segment of a Cineraria maritima leaf. This is the white leaf on the left of the picture.*

Coats Two mountain ash leaves, two sumach leaves, senecio greyii leaf, prunus leaf, middle section of a large raspberry leaf.

TRIMMINGS

Buttons Mimosa bobbles, senecio greyii buds, quaking grass.

Collars and cuffs Daisy petals, montbretia buds, anthemis daisy petal, pussy willow for fur collars and cuffs, statice florets.

Scarf Narrow delphinium petals, rudbeckia petals, anthemis daisy petals, narrow fuchsia petals.

Shoes Small leaflets of Virginia creeper, two end shoots of clematis montana, single honeysuckle flower (remove stamens), broom buds and seed pods, laburnum buds, montbretia buds, tiny piece of cow parsley leaf with a bit of stalk for a heel.

Handbags Rose petal, small senecio greyii leaf, pansy petal, tiny cotinus leaf, clary petal, rounded eccremocarpus leaf.

Handles Narrow fuchsia petal, small piece of stalk.

Clasp Mimosa bobble, statice floret, quaking grass.

Trousers Two cotinus leaves for plus-fours, two sumach leaves, two mountain ash leaves, two slim senecio greyii leaves, two willow leaves, part of a chestnut leaf.

Jackets Senecio greyii leaf, cotinus leaf, part of a chestnut leaf.

Hats Large clover head, larkspur floret, delphinium floret, fuchsia bud with seed box removed, buttercup petals, any small mal-pressed leaf, helichrysum flower, montbretia bud topped with a clary petal, piece of grass or odd bits of flowers for trimmings.

Umbrellas Virginia creeper leaflet, mountain ash leaflet, underside of a slim raspberry leaf, montana leaf, long slim fuchsia bud, Japanese maple leaf.

Parasol Same as for umbrella

Handles Any straight stalk, grass, montana, goosegrass, etc.

Ferrules Fuchsia seedbox, montbretia bud.

FISH

Bodies Senecio greyii leaves, rudbeckia petals, gazania petals, anthemis daisy petals, tulip petals, delphinium petals, poppy petals, honesty inner seed cases, cotinus leaf.

Tails End pair of clary bracts, inner petals of paeony, parrot tulip petals, Virginia creeper leaves, poppy petals.

Scales Honesty inner seed cases, potentilla petals.

Fins Horseshoe vetch florets, Virginia creeper leaves, silverweed, raspberry leaves.

Eyes Tiny senecio greyii leaves, orange cotoneaster leaves, broom seeds, muscari seeds, buttercup bud, quaking grass.

BIRDS

Bodies Senecio greyii leaf, ash or hornbeam leaf, bramble leaflet, sumach leaf, mountain ash leaf, prunus leaf.

Wings and tails Silverweed, part of herb Robert leaf, any narrow or folded autumn leaf, gaillardia petal.

Heads Senecio greyii, anthemis daisy centre, ox-eye daisy centre.

Beaks Horseshoe vetch floret, weigela bud, any piece of yellow petal.

Legs Piece of goosegrass stalk, piece of wisteria stalk, grass stalks.

Eyes As for fish.

Feet Rudbeckia petals, small end leaves of turkey oak with piece of stem attached, goosegrass leaflets, tiny sycamore leaves with piece of stem.

10 **POINTS TO REMEMBER**

DO . . .

. . . keep your work as clean as possible. A grubby finger mark can become an unplanned focal point!

. . . remember to remove the pollen from your flowers before covering them with glass, etc.

. . . press plenty of stalks.

. . . remember to change your pressing books around every few days or the material in the bottom books may become spotted with mildew.

. . . see that your finger-tip is really clean before rubbing off any blobs of glue.

. . . see that some of your stalks are pressed in a curve.

. . . use name tags in your pressing books. They can save you hours of searching.

. . . have a good supply of blotting paper or absorbent tissues.

. . . remember that your flowers will fade a little over the years and allow for this when choosing a background colour.

. . . remember that most green leaves turn brown when pressed. Some good pressers are listed on pages 19–20.

. . . cover your work and weight it down when you leave it, even if it is only for a few minutes.

. . . keep the windows closed when you are working. A sudden draught could send everything on the floor!

. . . remember to leave margins. Your work should never look cramped. Leave an extra wide margin on wall hangings, table mats etc, if you intend using coloured edging tape.

. . . keep your cartoons as simple as possible.

. . . paint wisteria and montana stalks with a mild disinfectant to stop mildew forming.

DON'T . . .

. . . stick down your design if you have any doubts about it. Put it right first.

. . . pick every flower in sight. Remember it is the design that matters, not the number of flowers.

. . . store your flowers in a damp or steamy room because they will lose their colour.

. . . keep your pressing books in too warm a room because the flowers will become brittle.

. . . pick flowers on a damp day.

. . . mount your pictures or cartoons. The flowers must be pressed right up against the glass to keep the petals from curling.

. . . press too heavily for too long a period. Allow your flowers occasional relief.

. . . be afraid to experiment with different flowers, leaves and new designs.

. . . use too much touch-up paint. Your flowers should look as natural as possible.

. . . use too much glue. Just a tiny dab here and there is all that is needed.

11 PRESSED FLOWER DECORATIONS FOR PROFIT

There is a growing demand for really first-class pressed flower decorations and though it is unlikely that you will make a full-time living from your skill, it is a pleasant and satisfying way of earning extra money. If you are really talented and enterprising, there is no knowing how far it will take you, but you must remember that the number of decorations you will be able to make will depend not only on the amount of time you have to spare, but also on the quantity of flowers you can press and store. Do build up a good stock of pictures, finger plates, lampshades etc. before offering them for sale. Your hobby will soon become a chore if you have to work at it all day long to cope with the orders. However, even if you have a large stock of pressed flowers it is a mistake to take on too many orders, unless you really want to turn your home into a factory. After a while it will become just plain hard work and your decorations will suffer, to say nothing of your health and temper! It is best to take on just enough work to fill your leisure time. Try not to sacrifice the hours you spend with your family and friends.

Once you decide that you would like to sell your work you must attract customers and build up a local reputation for your decorations. It is no good sitting at home waiting hopefully for friends to drop in and buy your work. You will not make any money that way. Go out and get your skill with pressed flowers known and talked about. Start by making a few of the smaller decorations, such as finger plates, wall hangings and table mats, for bazaars and bring and buy stalls, and tell clubs and societies about your work. You will not gain financially, but you will get some idea of what people are prepared to pay for your decorations, which designs sell best, the most popular colours, etc. This knowledge will be a great help when you start making decorations to sell.

HOW TO FIND CUSTOMERS

If you have built up a good stock of assorted decorations you can give an exhibition of your work in a local hall. Most towns have one of these halls which they keep just for exhibitions, and if you let it be known beforehand that you will be selling your decorations and accepting commissions, it can prove very rewarding indeed.

Another way is to approach your local handicraft and household shops. Take along some samples of your work to show the shopkeeper, and if they are attractive and well-made he will probably be only too pleased to give you an order on a sale-or-return basis. However, the profit on each decoration will not be large for the shop-keeper will want a fairly big percentage, but if you can maintain a reasonable flow of decorations throughout the year, you should have little difficulty in earning some extra money to help out the family budget.

You can also write to various people or organisations telling them that you are now making pressed flower decorations, and giving them full details of the type, size, price and delivery dates. This kind of letter is known as 'direct mail' and many small businesses find it the most effective method of advertising.

Should you feel that you would like to sell your work direct to your customers, you can put an advertisement in your local paper. If you do not know much about designing an advertisement, one of the paper's advertising staff will help. They will usually be glad to write and design it for you, at no extra expense. Always give your name, address and telephone number, if you have one—do not hide under a box number. People looking for Christmas or birthday presents are unlikely to go to the trouble of writing to ask when they may call and see your work. Make sure that the advertisement shows your hours of business and the amount charged for packing and postage.

Yet another way is to get your decorations some free publicity! Most newspapers have a Woman's Page and they are always on the lookout for interesting stories. A spare-time hobby that is becoming a flourishing little business is good news value, especially to a local newspaper. There is no need to wait until a paper approaches you, ring up the Features Editor and tell him about your decorations and how, for a small extra fee, a customer's own requirements can be met.

IN CONCLUSION

If your decorations are selling well, it is worth considering teaming up with others. Perhaps you could join up with someone whose hobby links up with yours. A friend who makes picture frames might make the frames for the pictures you produce, another could make lampshades for you to decorate. But whatever you decide, be businesslike. Keep a strict account of all expenditure to set against profits, organize your work carefully, and if you promise an order by a certain date, make sure you keep to it.

If you enjoy making pressed flower decorations and have the talent and the flowers, it can be a pretty good way of making some extra money. There will be problems of course, such as finding room to store all your flowers, and the rush to get all your other work done so that you can pick and press while the sun is shining, but, if you have common sense and unlimited energy, these problems can be overcome. After all, there is almost no easy way of making money. If there were, everybody would be doing it.

All the same, making pressed flower decorations is a happy and satisfying way of earning a little extra, and these days every little helps a lot!

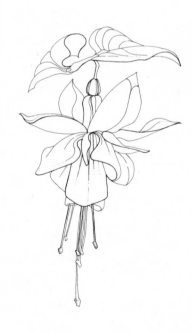

APPENDIX

Listed below are the biological equivalents of the common names used in the text

ash	*Fraxinus excelsior*	lavender	*Lavandula spica*
aspen	*Populus tremula*	London pride	*Saxfraga umbrosa*
barley	*Hordeum*	mallow, common	*Malvaceae*
barren brome	*Bromus sterilis*	maple	*Acer campestre*
beech	*Fagus sylvatica*	mimosa	*Acacia decurrens*
Bermuda grass	*Cynodon dactylon*	montbretia	*Crocosmia*
blackberry	*Rubus fruticosus*	mountain ash	*Sorbus aucuparia*
bramble	*Rubus fruticosus*	nipplewort	*Lapsana cummunis*
broom	*Cytisus scoparius*	oak	*Quercus*
buttercup	*Ranunculus*	old-man's-beard	*Clematis vitalba*
celandine, lesser	*Ranunculus ficaria*	ox-eye daisy	*Buphthalum salicifolium*
chestnut	*Aesculus*	pansy	*Viola tricolor hortensis*
Christmas rose	*Helleborus niger*	pasque flower	*Pulsatilla vulgaris*
cinquefoil	*Potentilla reptens*	passion flower	*Passiflora caerulea*
clary	*Salvia sclarea*	poppy	*Papaver rhoeas*
clover	*Trifolium*	primrose	*Primula vulgaris*
cosmos	*Cosmea*	pussy willow	*Salix discolor*
cow parsley	*Anthriscus sylvestris*	quaking grass	*Briza media*
daffodil	*Narcissus*	raspberry	*Rubus idaeus*
daisy	*Bellis perennis*	silverweed	*Potentilla anserina*
fennel	*Foeniculum vulgare*	spring cinquefoil	*Potentilla tabernaemontani*
goosegrass	*Galium aparine*	statice	*Limonum*
heather	*Erica scinerea*	sumach	*Rhus*
herb Robert	*Geranium robertianum*	sycamore	*Acer pseudoplatanus*
honesty	*Lunaria annua*	tormentil	*Potentilla ereta*
honeysuckle	*Lonicera*	trefoil	*Trifolium*
hornbeam	*Carpinus betulus*	Turkey oak	*Quercus cerris*
horseshoe	*Hippocrepis comosa*	Virginia creeper	*Parthenocissus*
Japanese maple	*Acer japonicum*	weeping willow	*Salix alba tristis*
ladies bedstraw	*Galium verum*	wild parsnip	*Pastinaca sativa*
larkspur	*Delphinium ajacis*	woodruff	*Galium odoratum*

INDEX